A Walk Through The Pilgrim's Progress
with Dr. Daniel Dongwon Lee

A Walk Through The Pilgrim's Progress
with Dr. Daniel Dongwon Lee

Copyright ⓒ 2018 by Daniel Dongwon Lee
All rights reserved.

Published by Duranno Ministry
Phone : +82-2-2078-3331
Email : tpress@duranno.com
Home Page : www.duranno.com
Address : 38, Seobinggo-ro 65-gil, Yongsan-gu, Seoul, Republic of Korea

Originally Published in Korean under the title : "이동원 목사와 함께 걷는 천로역정"
Copyright ⓒ 2016 by Duranno Ministry

This edition is published by permission of Daniel Dongwon Lee. No part of this book may be reproduced in any form without written permission from the publisher, except in the case of brief quotations embodied in critical articles and reviews.

All Scripture quotations, unless otherwise indicated, are taken from the New International Version 2011.

ISBN 978-89-531-3083-8 03230
printed in korea

A Walk Through
The Pilgrim's Progress
with Dr. Daniel Dongwon Lee

Daniel Dongwon Lee

Translated by
Lifespring Translation Team

Duranno

Table of Contents

Preface Message from *The Pilgrim's Progress* for the Postmodern Generation | 6

1 We Are All Pilgrims [Heb. 11:13-16] | 11
2 Spirituality of The Pilgrim's Progress [Heb. 12:1-2] | 21
3 Benefits of Suffering [Ps. 119:67, 71] | 31
4 Seeker [Acts 2:37] | 45
5 Evangelist [Matt. 3:7, 7:13-14] | 57
6 Types of Seekers [Matt. 13:1-9] | 69
7 The Wicket Gate [Matt. 7:7, 7:13-14] | 83
8 The Hill of the Cross [Luke 23:33-34, 42-43] | 97
9 The Interpreter [1 Cor. 3:1, 4:15] | 109
10 Spiritual Direction [1 Thess. 2:6b-8, 11-12] | 121
11 Sleeping Man [Prov 5:22-23, 6:9] | 135
12 Hill Difficulty [2 Cor. 1:3-7] | 147
13 House Beautiful [1 Tim. 3:15] | 159

14 Blessing of Peace (Rom. 5:1-2) | 171

15 Blessing of Faith (Heb. 11:1-3) | 183

16 Blessing of Putting On Spiritual Armor (Eph. 6:10-13) | 197

17 Valley of Humiliation (2 Cor. 12:7-10) | 211

18 Valley of the Shadow of Death (Ps. 23:4) | 225

19 Faithful and Talkative (1 Cor. 4:15-21) | 237

20 Vanity Fair (Eccles. 1:1-2, 12:13-14) | 251

21 Lesson of Demas (2 Tim. 4:10, Gen. 19:26) | 263

22 Prison of Despair (Acts 12:1-10) | 275

23 Delectable Mountains (Ezek. 34:12-16) | 289

24 Ignorance and Little Faith (Gal. 2:11-16, 3:1-3) | 303

25 Enchanted Ground (1 Thess. 5:1-11) | 317

26 The Land of Beulah (Isa. 62:1-5) | 329

27 River of Death and New Jerusalem (Isa. 43:1-7, Rev. 21:1-2) | 343

Notes | 354

Preface

Message from *The Pilgrim's Progress* for the Postmodern Generation

The Pilgrim's Progress is a Christian classic. Classics are old yet always new. That is because their message transcends time. In every place the Bible was introduced, this book was the next to be translated. That is why *The Pilgrim's Progress* is introduced as the most read book after the Bible.

The Pilgrim's Progress has also been a reservoir of sermons for protestant ministers. This book was a source of inspiration for Charles Spurgeon, the "Prince of Preachers." For Rev. Sun Joo Gil, this book was the reason for his conversion.[1] To Rev. Sung

Bong Lee, this book was a central theme for his revival meetings.² After I became a Christian, a missionary gave me this book as a gift, which became the foundation of my faith.

In September 2016, we opened the Pilgrim's Progress Pilgrimage Park at Pilgrim House. Before this project, I reread *The Pilgrim's Progress* more than ten times. I also did a year-long expository preaching series on *The Pilgrim's Progress*. This book is being published as we celebrate the opening of the Pilgrim's Progress Pilgrimage Park because I believe that today's postmodern audience especially needs to hear the message of this book.

I want to bless the postmodern generation reading this book and pray that you will read the original *The Pilgrim's Progress* as well. And please do make a visit to the Pilgrim's Progress Pilgrimage Park in Gapyeong, Korea.³ If this book can help solidify the foundation of our faith, that will be pleasing to the Author and Perfecter of our faith.

I pray that all of us reading this book will finish strong the journey of pilgrimage ahead of us.

I would like to express my appreciation to Lifespring Translation Team and Duranno publishing company.

Your Fellow Pilgrim,

Dr. Daniel Dongwon Lee

Hebrews 11:13-16

All these people were still living by faith when they died. They did not receive the things promised; they only saw them and welcomed them from a distance. And they admitted that they were aliens and strangers on earth. People who say such things show that they are looking for a country of their own. If they had been thinking of the country they had left, they would have had opportunity to return. Instead, they were longing for a better country – a heavenly one. Therefore, God is not ashamed to be called their God, for he has prepared a city for them.

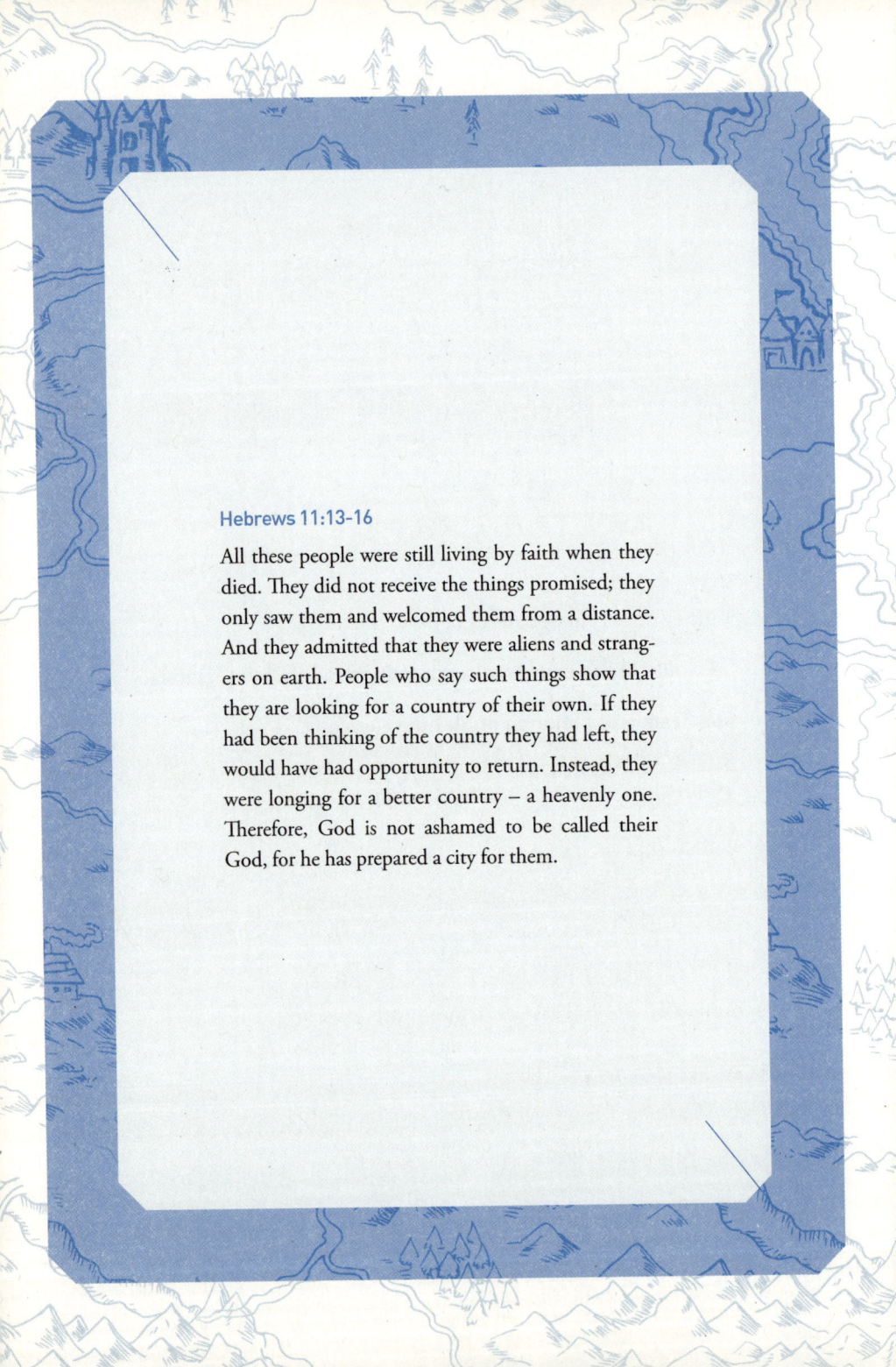

Pilgrim's Progress 1

We Are All Pilgrims

Wanderers on the Earth

I have had several occasions to visit Jeju Island. Jeju is an island that gave Koreans the opportunity for overseas travel when the country was closed to other countries. Historically, Jeju was called an island of triple disasters – water, drought, and wind. During the Yi Chosun Dynasty, the island was used as a place of exile for political losers. But ever since Jeju was designated as a UNESCO World Natural Heritage Site in 2007, and visa-free travel became possible, the beautiful island now attracts many foreign tourists. In 2013, the yearly number of tourists exceeded 10 million.

I talked with an administrative official in Jeju and heard that although the increase in visits is a prosperous blessing to Jeju, it has also led to more challenges due to rude tourists. Hebrews 11:13-16 says that Christians are "strangers" and "pilgrims" on this earth. We are here as pilgrims.

As I read the passage, I started to think, "What kind of pilgrim life am I living on this earth?" The moment we accept Jesus as Savior and Lord, we become citizens of the Kingdom of God. We live our lives as foreigners and wanderers on this earth. That is because we are pilgrims on this earth.

If there is a book that challenges Christians to live as beautiful pilgrims on this earth, it is *The Pilgrim's Progress*, the most read book after the Bible. This book was written by John Bunyan, an English Baptist. In September 2016, the "Pilgrim's Progress Pilgrimage Park" opened at Gapyeong Pilgrim House in Korea as a sculpture park. It is now used as a spiritual pilgrimage learning site for Christians all over the world.

I would like to share the secret to living a beautiful pilgrim life during our temporary stay on earth through Hebrews 11.

The Beautiful Life's Journey of a Pilgrim

First, we must believe in the reality of our heavenly home. True pilgrims know their ultimate home. The Bible teaches that this home is in heaven. If we live our lives without knowing this home, we are not pilgrims but wandering wayfarers. We must ask ourselves if we are pilgrims or wayfarers.

> "Instead, they were longing for a better country – a heavenly one. Therefore God is not ashamed to be called their God, for he has prepared a city for them"(Heb. 11:16).

The other name for our heavenly home is the city God has prepared for his people. John Bunyan calls this city "Mountain Zion." This place, also called "Celestial City" or "New Jerusalem," is the ultimate home believers look forward to.

All mankind has their own home country on this earth. For some that is China, for others it is America, Japan, Mongolia, or Southeast Asia. And for many reading this book, it is Korea. The father of our faith, Abraham's home country was Ur of the Chaldeans. But Abraham and his descendants did not long to return to their hometown.

> "If they had been thinking of the country they had left, they would have had opportunity to return" (Heb. 11:15).

In verse 16, it says they were "longing for a better country." Now all Christians who have been saved have one home – that is our heavenly home.

> "But our citizenship is in heaven. And we eagerly await a Savior from there, the Lord Jesus Christ" (Phil. 3:20).

We have become citizens of the Kingdom of God and also pilgrims in this world. This is our new identity. Our identity is secure as we believe in our eternal home in heaven. Our predecessors of the faith lived believing in heaven and died believing in it. It is difficult to experience the full glory of heaven in this world. That is why verse 13 says that "they did not receive the things promised." Rather they "only saw them and welcomed them from a distance." We must believe in the reality of our eternal home and walk the pilgrim's path daily.

Second, we must walk together in a pilgrim community.
In verse 13, it is not an individual that walks the pilgrimage but

the plural "people" or "they." This means that there are people walking with them as companions along the way. In *The Pilgrim's Progress*, an important factor for Christian to complete the pilgrimage was the presence of companions that are on the journey with him. In the first half, Faithful is his companion and in the latter half, Hopeful joins him. When Faithful is martyred at Vanity Fair, Hopeful is the one who witnesses the event and is touched by it. Hopeful walks with Christian until they enter Celestial City. It is an incredible blessing to have these companions on our journey to Celestial City. The Christian life is not meant to be done alone. I believe that the Korean church must become a friend to foreign believers living in this country as aliens.

Perhaps John Bunyan thought that a single friend could not guarantee the completion of pilgrimage, so he brings a community. In *The Pilgrim's Progress*, we can see House Beautiful. Here we meet believers such as Discretion, Prudence, Piety, and Charity and are encouraged by them. At House Beautiful, Christian enjoys the blessing of fellowship with believers, and it is there he is spiritually armed. This is the purpose of the church community. Along the pilgrimage path, Christian also reaches the Delectable Mountains. This mountain is also nicknamed the land of Immanuel. While he rests, Christian meets four shepherds. Their names are Knowledge, Experience, Watchful, and Sincere. With their guidance and teaching, Christian gains new strength to walk the pilgrim's path again. This is what a true church community should look like. I pray that our churches become such pilgrim communities.

Third, we should live the life of a pilgrim seeking our real home.

As our predecessors confessed, we live as aliens and pilgrims in this world. After we become Christians, our entire life becomes a pilgrimage journey to find our real home.

> "People who say such things show that they are looking for a country of their own" (Heb. 11:14).

What does it mean to "look for a country of their own?" This means that the person who only knows life in this world and the person who looks for the heavenly home lead completely different lives. If a wayfarer is too obsessed with what is on the way, his pilgrimage cannot help but be distracted. That is why the Bible tells us, "Do not love the world or anything in the world. If anyone loves the world, the love of the Father is not in him" (1 John 2:15).

The next verse shows what the world's values consist of.

> "For everything in the world – the cravings of sinful man, the lust of his eyes and the boasting of what he has and does – comes not from the Father but from the world" (1 John 2:16).

In *The Pilgrim's Progress*, Christian and Faithful reach Vanity Fair. Everything sold and bought in this market is meaningless. They all arouse the cravings of sinful man, the lust of his eyes, and the boasting of what he has and does. There are products from many different countries. Christian and Faithful must go through this street and market to reach New Jerusalem. The two pilgrims pray as they walk by the street of displays.

> "Turn my eyes away from worthless things" (Ps. 119:37).

One merchant asks the two pilgrims who express no interest in the goods on sale in the market, "What are you looking for? What do you want to buy?"

The two pilgrims answer, "We want to buy the truth" (Prov. 23:23).

Their ultimate interest is "truth." With this answer they demonstrate that they are seeking their true home. Because of this answer

Faithful pays the price of martyrdom. But they do not fear these obstacles of hardship. They are pilgrims seeking their home. They believe that they will arrive home soon.

There was a missionary, Henry Morrison, who served in Africa for 40 years. He was returning to America on a boat to the New York harbor with his wife. On that boat was also President Teddy Roosevelt, who was returning from a hunting vacation in Africa. As the ship arrived in the harbor, there was a red carpet and trumpet sounds from the military band to welcome the president. When the president left the harbor, so did the red carpet and the trumpet sounds. As Henry Morrison made his way out onto the bare harbor, he complained to God.

"God, did you see the welcoming for the president returning from hunting? How come there is no welcoming for me, after working 40 years for you?"

Right then Henry Morrison heard a voice from heaven.

"Henry, you are not home yet!"

I bless all of us, that we would live as pilgrims of faith, living each day looking forward to our heavenly home. I hope we become pilgrims of faith looking forward to our heavenly home through John Bunyan's *The Pilgrim's Progress*.

Questions for the Pilgrimage of Faith

1. Read John Bunyan's *The Pilgrim's Progress*.

2. Summarize the three secrets to walk the journey of life as a beautiful pilgrim.
   1)
   2)
   3)

3. If you were to go through Vanity Fair, what would you be most tempted by? What can you do to overcome that temptation?

4. Do you look forward to your heavenly home daily? What do you think it means to live a life looking forward to our home?

Hebrews 12:1-2

Therefore, since we are surrounded by such a great cloud of witnesses, let us throw off everything that hinders and the sin that so easily entangles, and let us run with perseverance the race marked out for us. Let us fix our eyes on Jesus, the author and perfecter of our faith, who for the joy set before him endured the cross, scorning its shame, and sat down at the right hand of the throne of God.

Pilgrim's Progress 2

Spirituality of The Pilgrim's Progress

Pilgrim's Progress Pilgrimage Park

In celebration of our 20-year anniversary, Global Mission Church decided to undertake a meaningful project for Korean Church history and make Pilgrim's Progress Pilgrimage Park at Pilgrim House in Gapyeong, Korea. We finished this project in September 2016, and this sculpture park will be used for people who wish to walk and meditate on the meaning of life and faith.

There are a few tabernacle replicas in Korea and many Catholic

Stations of the Cross worldwide, but, as far as I know, this is the first Pilgrim's Progress Pilgrimage Park in history that has been established. As *The Pilgrim's Progress* is the most read book after the Bible and largely represents the Protestant faith, this pilgrimage park will provide a meaningful experience for Christians worldwide. As such, guided tours are available not only in Korean, but also in English, Chinese, and Japanese.

The spiritual significances taught by *The Pilgrim's Progress* will create a historical legacy for the future of the Korean church. By examining the types of spiritualities in *The Pilgrim's Progress*, we will meditate on what essential spiritualities we must build the future of the Korean church. What are the core spiritualities we can learn through *The Pilgrim's Progress*?

Core Spiritualities of Christianity

First is the spirituality of salvation.

Hebrews 12:1 describes the Christian life as a "race." To complete this race in victory, verse 2 encourages us to "fix our eyes on Jesus, the author and perfecter of our faith." Here, the NIV translation describes Jesus as the Author and Perfecter. This means that Jesus alone is the one that helps us start this race of faith and also helps us complete this race.

Jesus is the beginning and the end of our faith, the Alpha and the Omega. When we meet Jesus personally and believe in Him as our Lord and Savior, we experience salvation. Salvation is a gift we receive when we place our faith in Jesus as our Savior. The Bible promises, "Believe in the Lord Jesus, and you will be saved -- you and your household"(Acts 16:31).

In 2014, Korea experienced the great tragedy of the Sewol ferry incident.[4] Along with the 304 innocent lives that were sacrificed, we must not look over the fact that this incident downgraded the biblical truth of salvation to a joke, making it a laughingstock. The problem with the community of faith that was at the center of this incident is the false teaching on salvation. Instead of teaching a biblical and personal doctrine of salvation by faith, they falsely taught salvation as a spiritual realization that could only be experienced within their exclusive community.

But this is not what salvation is. Salvation is so important. You must receive it. Hebrews 2:3 clearly says, "How shall we escape if we ignore such a great salvation?"(emphasis added). The greatest doctrinal issue that Bunyan's *The Pilgrim's Progress* addresses is the doctrine of salvation. Christian, the main character of *The Pilgrim's*

Progress, enters the scene wearing rags with a book in his hand and a heavy burden on his back. While reading the Bible, the book of books, he is convicted in his heart and cries out "What shall I do?"

With Evangelist's help, Christian makes his way through the Wicket Gate and finally stands before the Hill of the Cross. At last, he is free from the heavy burden on his back. Three angels appear before him and each relay an important message. The first angel declares, "Your sins are forgiven." The second strips him of his rags and clothes him with a new garment. Finally, the last angel places a mark on his forehead. This is the essence of the salvation experience. At the moment we believe in Jesus, who died on the cross for us and rose again, as Lord and Savior, we are forgiven of our sins, called righteous, and marked as a child of God. This is salvation. *The Pilgrim's Progress* clearly and vividly relays this spirituality of salvation.

Second is the spirituality of sanctification.
As we saw earlier, meeting Jesus on our life's pilgrimage, accepting Him as Lord and Savior, and being saved is an amazing incident that is incomparable with anything else. Yet the confession of salvation is not the end of our faith; it is only the beginning. After entering the Wicket Gate and experiencing the cross, Christian

faces a long journey full of hardships. This is the other spirituality of *The Pilgrim's Progress* -- the spirituality of sanctification.

The part where Christian reads the Bible and starts his journey as a seeker and reaches the Hill of the Cross is only 20 percent of the entire plot of *The Pilgrim's Progress*. The task he has for the remaining 80 percent is to become holy through the journey of sanctification.

> "Therefore, since we are surrounded by such a great cloud of witnesses, let us throw off everything that hinders and the sin that so easily entangles"(Heb. 12:1).

Is throwing off everything that hinders and the sin that so easily entangles the endpoint of our faith? No, the Bible says the following.

> "…and let us run with perseverance the race marked out for us"(Heb. 12:1).

Our salvation is receiving the grace of forgiveness of sins. But does this mean that all sins have departed from us? To be saved, we must turn our life's direction from a life without God to a life that is fixated upon and reliant on God. This is fundamental repentance. However, salvation is not the end of repentance, rather the start. For the rest of our lives, we must continue to turn from sins that displease the Lord. Our journey of faith is a continuous fight against sin.

> "In your struggle against sin, you have not yet resisted to the point of shedding your blood" (Heb. 12:4).

This struggle against sin, in which we stumble at times and experience victories at times, is the journey of sanctification. *The Pilgrim's Progress* paints a vivid picture of this process. Christian goes through the Valley of Humiliation, passes through the Valley of the Shadow of Death, experiences difficulty at Vanity Fair, is imprisoned in the Prison of Despair, all to finally be transformed into the bride of Christ. This is the journey of sanctification.

Third is the spirituality of finishing the race.
The last thing that awaits Christian in *The Pilgrim's Progress* is the River of Death. The pilgrim asks if there is any other way to enter Celestial City. The angels answer, "There is no other way. You must go through, or you cannot come at the gate of Zion." Once the pilgrims set foot in the river, the river becomes deeper and deeper.

The angels tell them that the water level will change depending on how much they trust the King of the river, the King of both this side and that side of the river.

Whenever Christian is about to sink with fear in the water, Hopeful shouts, "Brother, I see the gate, and men standing by to receive us."

Relying on the Word that "when you pass through the waters, I will be with you; and when you pass through the rivers, they will not sweep over you"(Isa. 43:2), Christian and Hopeful finally enter Celestial City.

The final spirituality required for pilgrims is the spirituality of finishing the race. This honor is given to those who trust that Jesus is the only one who makes it possible to finish the race and run the race with their eyes fixed on Him. This is the glory of finishing the race.

> "Let us fix our eyes on Jesus, the author and perfecter of our faith, who for the joy set before him endured the cross, scorning its shame, and sat down at the right hand of the throne of God"(Heb. 12:2).

Jesus, who endured the cross, scorning its shame, and sat down at the right hand of the throne of God is the ultimate model for us to look at for this race of faith. If we continue to fix our eyes on Jesus, by God's grace, we too will sit at the right hand of the throne of God. This is the day our race is completed. We must look forward to this day with hope and anticipation.

I truly hope that all of us will finish this race. I pray that the Pilgrim's Progress Pilgrimage Park is used as a blessed tool to teach the spirituality of finishing the race.

Questions for the Pilgrimage of Faith

1. What are the three main spiritualities that Bunyan emphasizes in *The Pilgrim's Progress*?
1)
2)
3)

2. Out of the three spiritualities mentioned in this chapter, which one do you need the most?

3. What are you doing to be victorious in the battle against sin and to fix your eyes on God?

4. In order to finish this race of faith, what do you need to focus on?

Psalm 119:67

Before I was afflicted I went astray, but now I obey your word.

Psalm 119:71

It was good for me to be afflicted so that I might learn your decrees.

Pilgrim's Progress 3

Benefits of Suffering

The Great Psalm 119

One frequently asked question at Bible quiz competitions in church is "what is the longest chapter in the Bible?" The answer is, of course, Psalm 119. It is easy to answer, but it is difficult to read every verse of Psalm 119. Although this psalm is very well-known, the entire chapter is not well-read. Despite this fact, Psalm 119 is called "The Great Psalm." Why do you think this is?

First of all, as stated above, it is known for being the longest chapter in the Bible. There is a total of 176 verses in this chapter. For reference, the Hebrew alphabet has 22 letters, and in this psalm there are 8 verses for each letter, resulting in 176 verses total.

Secondly, it is a beautiful poem with various literary expressions, including thanksgiving, supplications, confessions, poems, praises, lamentations, joy, wisdom, and many more that describe life's ups and downs.

Thirdly, the most amazing praise for the Word of God is written in this psalm. God's Word is described as the law, statutes, promises, commands, precepts, decrees, deeds, discernment, and testimonies in this psalm.

Lastly, this Psalm is called "The Great Psalm" because it not only praises the Word but also testifies to believers about the practical benefits of the Word in times of suffering.

> "I have suffered much; preserve my life, LORD, according to your word" (Ps. 119:107).

> "Though I constantly take my life in my hands, I will not forget your law" (Ps. 119:109).

> "Trouble and distress have come upon me, but your commands

give me delight"(Ps. 119:143).

However, Psalm 119:67 and 71, verses that testify about the most amazing benefits of such difficulties in life, are regarded as true gems within all of Psalm 119. Additionally, one of the famous lovers of this psalm is John Bunyan, the author of *The Pilgrim's Progress*. Together, let us consider the road of adversity in *The Pilgrim's Progress* and the benefits of suffering.

Benefits of Suffering

First, suffering is an instrument God uses to sanctify our lives.

I believe that the Israelites and Koreans, among the many nations on Earth, are two nations that have experienced an incredibly large number of difficulties and have been drawn closer to God in the process. According to Korean historians, Korea has gone through approximately 900 major and minor wars with foreign countries since it was established. We have experienced a war almost every 7 years. Finally, we experienced the Korean War, a globally known and historically well-documented war. Early Christian thinker,

Sok Hon Ham, explains the meaning of the Korean War in his book, *Queen of Suffering: A Spiritual History of Korea.*

> "Now this land of beauty has become the world's public graveyard. … This country has become an altar of humanity, the UN, and the National Alliance. As Abraham sacrificed his son on the altar and all the ancestors of nations came from that son, now humanity offers its son and sacrifices him as an offering for the new generation, new nation, and new race."

Sok Hon Ham calls our national history a "history of suffering" and our nation the "Queen of Suffering." In fact, before the Korean War, Korea was struggling with extreme ideological confrontations due to the lack of control over their own freedom after the Japanese occupation. Even churches in Korea were suffering from divisions due to ecumenical conflicts. However, after the Korean War, we were able to seek revival for the country and a new history for the church. This became the foundation for modern Korean history. The difficulties of war had given a new face to the Queen of Suffering.

The most amazing gift given by this history of passion is testified clearly in Psalm 119.

> "Before I was afflicted I went astray, but now I obey your word" (Verse 67).

Regarding this point, John Bunyan was someone who experienced the truth of this verse through the difficulties in his life. John Bunyan was born in 1628, in the village of Elstow near Bedfordshire, England to a poor tinker. He had to fight against difficulties to survive from a very young age. At that time, even poor people could improve their lives if they received proper education, but Bunyan only managed to afford basic elementary education. Later, in 1644, his mother passed away when he was sixteen, and he enlisted in the Parliamentary army that year due to the breakout of the English Civil War between the Parliamentarians and the Royalists. He witnessed the horrors of war during his two-and-a-half years of military service.

However, through these hardships, he drew closer and closer to God. Soon after in 1649 at the age of 21, he married a young woman. His wife was poor, but devout in her faith and recommended two books to Bunyan. They were *The Plain Man's Pathway to Heaven* by Arthur Dent and *The Practice of Piety* by Lewis Bayly. As he read these books, he was strongly drawn to God's Word. The suffering in his adolescence was God's instrument to make

Bunyan's life holy.

Second, suffering is an instrument that teaches us God's Word.

The psalmist confesses in Psalm 119:17 that suffering not only corrects the unrighteous path of life, but also teaches us the Word of God concretely.

> "It was good for me to be afflicted so that I might learn your decrees."

After the Korean War, our nation struggled through poverty and starvation in the land made desolate by the Korean War. However, what was stronger than our physical hunger was our spiritual hunger. People gathered at church every day to listen to His Word, enduring the pain of hunger. From Monday to Friday, the revival services held early in the morning, at noon, and at night were crowded with people. Vacation Bible Schools were completely packed with children. It was during this period that many Christians desired to read the entire Bible and did so, day and night. God spoke to our nation very powerfully through Amos 8:11.

> "'The days are coming,' declares the Sovereign Lord, 'when I will send a famine through the land—not a famine of food or a thirst for water, but a famine of hearing the words of the Lord.'"

Also, the most familiar hymns to us were given during that time. The Korean War gave birth to the hymns of our nation.

> "Sing them over again to me, wonderful words of life; let me more of their beauty see, wonderful words of life; words of life and beauty, teach me faith and duty: Beautiful words, wonderful words, wonderful words of life."

> "Father, I stretch my hands to Thee, no other help I know; if Thou withdraw Thyself from me, ah! Whither shall I go? I do believe, I now believe that Jesus died for me. And that He shed His precious blood from sin to set me free."

> "Nearer, my God, to Thee, nearer to Thee! E'en though it be a cross that raiseth me, still all my song shall be, nearer, my God, to Thee. Nearer, my God, to Thee, nearer to Thee!"

> "I am coming to the cross; I am poor and weak and blind; I am

counting all but dross; I shall full salvation find. I am trusting the Lord, in Thee, Blessed Lamb of Calvary; humbly at Thy cross I bow, save me Jesus, save me now."

"I'm pressing on the upward way, new heights I'm gaining everyday; still praying as I onward bound, 'Lord, plant my feet on higher ground.' Lord, lift me up, and let me stand by faith on Canaan's table and; a higher plane than I have found, Lord, plant my feet on higher ground."

Some people call these hymns the Five Hymns of our nation. When we walk through the valley of suffering, we should draw closer to Jesus as we sing these hymns and press on, step by step, toward the Word spoken to us from the Lord.

Suffering is a classroom in the wilderness that teaches us the Word of God. John Bunyan testifies to this statement. In his biography, 12 year-old Bunyan had a near death experience as his boat overturned while he was playing with his friend on the Ouse River in Bedfordshire. Fortunately, someone who happened to be passing by rescued him and his friend. At that moment, he came to understand what it means to have a grateful heart towards someone for the first time in his life.

Soon after that incident, he nearly died from being bitten by a poisonous snake. When his friend shouted to him, "John, there is a poisonous snake right under your foot!" Bunyan jumped up in shock and moved out of the way. At that moment, he felt as if someone had lifted him up and moved him. John Bunyan recalls that he experienced the existence of the Almighty One who saved him twice.

Later when his mother passed away, he had to face the truth that everyone dies in the end for the first time in his life. Also he started asking, "Is life all about being buried after death?" He remembered his mother saying, "There is eternal life after death," and began to seriously ponder her words.

After that, he enlisted and experienced another amazing incident in his life. One day, it was his turn to be on sentry duty, but he was suffering from body aches and a fever. His fellow soldier saw this and offered to switch with him for their rotation. That night, the soldier was shot to death by an infiltrated enemy. This incident became a very important memory in his life as it helped him understand the biblical concept of atonement: "I came to life because someone else died on my behalf." Due to this incident, John Bunyan started his life journey as a serious seeker of truth after he was discharged from the army. As stated in this psalm, he experienced the truth and provisions of God through the difficulties.

> "It was good for me to be afflicted so that I might learn your decrees" (Ps. 119:71).

John Bunyan repented and became zealous for the truth of the Gospel. As a layperson, he started sharing the Word and giving testimonies. However, according to the Act of State Religion in England, it was illegal for unordained laymen (unlicensed preachers) to preach. When he was arrested for preaching the Gospel, he defended himself in court.

> "If I am persecuted and afflicted for the gospel I preach, I consider this a gracious opportunity from the Lord. I am grateful to be arrested for doing the good work of Heaven as a man of God. I hope you know it is rather a blessing to suffer for the Lord."

For preaching the Gospel, Bunyan spent 12 years in prison. How did he handle such false accusations and undeserved imprisonment? In his memoir, he recalls:

> "I never had in all my life so great an inlet into the Word of God

as now; those Scriptures that I saw nothing in before, are made in this place and state to shine upon me; Jesus Christ also was never more real and apparent than now; here I have seen and felt him indeed⋯ for look how fears have presented themselves, so have supports and encouragements; yea, when I have started, even as it were at nothing else but my shadow, yet God, as being very tender to me, hath not suffered me to be molested, but would, with one scripture or another, strengthen me against all; insomuch that I have often said, Were it lawful, I could pray for greater trouble, for the greater comfort's sake⋯ Hebrews 13:6 lifted me up throughout the imprisonment. 'The Lord is my helper; I will not be afraid. What can mere mortals do to me?'"

He read the Bible and *Foxe's Book of Martyrs* while he was in jail. Thanks to his intimate fellowship with God, John Bunyan had a joyful and grace-filled prison time and was able to write *The Pilgrim's Progress*, the most read book after the Bible and the most significant work of Christian literature. Famous poet Robert Browning made a statement regarding this book:

"A fiery tear he put in every tone. 'Tis my belief God spoke; no tinker has such powers."

Again we can only say "amen" before this psalm.

> "It was good for me to be afflicted so that I might learn your decrees" (Ps. 119:71).

For those who are walking in the valley of suffering today and for people of faith who are on the path of *The Pilgrim's Progress*, I pray for Jesus to be with you and the grace of His Words to be upon you.

Questions for the Pilgrimage of Faith

1. List out the two benefits of suffering.

1)

2)

2. Discuss how the difficulties that John Bunyan faced benefited him.

3. What kinds of difficulties have you experienced in the journey of life? Recollect how those difficulties have benefited you.

4. What are the truths and provisions of God that you have learned when you face difficulties in life? Have you had a moment where you could thank Him for the difficulties?

Acts 2:37

When the people heard this, they were cut to the heart and said to Peter and the other apostles, "Brothers, what shall we do?"

> Pilgrim's Progress 4

Seeker

Walking the Camino de Santiago

A few years ago, I read a book called *I Followed the Yellow Arrow*. Even though I did not know the author, I was drawn by the title of the book. These days many more people walk the pilgrimage to Santiago, and this book has taken part in prompting people to go. I, too, was able to visit Santiago.

Camino de Santiago is a pilgrimage road towards Santiago de Compostela, a city in Northwest Spain. This is where the graveyard of James(according to Spain Catholics), one of Jesus' twelve disciples known as the guardian saint of Spain, is located.

Even at this moment, many people with scallop shells on their backpacks are walking the 800 km-long road, following the yellow arrows. For what purpose do they walk this road? Perhaps each of them will have a different reason. Some of them may be looking for their lost self, some may simply be looking for rest, and some may be seeking to meet God. However, if we were to call them by a common name, it would be "Seeker of Truth." Everyone is seeking the way, the ultimate answer for life.

Young Eun Seo, the author of *I Followed the Yellow Arrow*, was the third wife of Dong Li Kim, a poet and novelist. She is a famous writer who made a surprise debut in literary circles and won the Yi Sang Literary Award(the 7th) in her thirties. She began her pilgrimage journey at the age of 66, writing her will before her departure. On the pilgrimage road, she encountered God and wrote about the outcome of her pilgrimage walk as follows:

> "I have become a completely different person. I witnessed and touched the transcendental being that transformed my inner self."

She had called herself Christian for 17 years before this experience, yet she was a nominal Christian who had never encountered God. Strictly speaking, she was a Christian seeking the Truth.

Young Eun Seo's book on being a seeker is very inspiring, but there is a book written long before hers that marks the peak of seeker literature. It is John Bunyan's *The Pilgrim's Progress*. At the start of his journey, the protagonist of this book is given the name Christian. However, he still has to walk through many paths before he becomes a true Christian. More precisely, he is a seeker from the moment he leaves his home. He is a very sincere seeker. Today's generation is a generation that has lost the spirit of being a true seeker. To this generation, I would like to explore how we can become earnest truth seekers by looking at the journey of Christian, the protagonist of *The Pilgrim's Progress*.

Preparation to Become an Earnest Seeker

First, we have to listen to the Word of Heaven.
Theology teaches that the Word of Heaven, or the Word of God, is a "special revelation" from God. The Word of revelation, which God uses to reveal Himself to humanity in a special way, is the Bible. In *The Pilgrim's Progress*, many Bible verses appear. John

Bunyan encountered God through these very verses. In fact, the introduction of the book begins as follows:

> "As I walked through the wilderness of this world, I lighted on a certain place where was a den, and laid me down in that place to sleep; and as I slept, I dreamed a dream. I dreamed, and behold, I saw a man clothed with rags, standing in a certain place, with his face from his own house, a book in his hand, and a great burden upon his back. I looked, and saw him open the book, and read therein; and as he read, he wept and trembled; and, not being able longer to contain, he brake out with a lamentable cry, saying, 'What shall I do?'"

At the end of the quote, he asks, "What shall I do?" This question is quoted from Acts 2:37.

> "When the people heard this, they were cut to the heart and said to Peter and the other apostles, 'Brothers, what shall we do?'"

This was the outcry of confession from about 120 Christians who were praying together in Mark's attic on the day of Pentecost. The Holy Spirit came upon them and touched their hearts as they were listening to Apostle Peter, who was filled with the Holy Spirit and preaching the Word. This was the moment when the early Christians experienced the Holy Spirit's presence for the first time and encountered the Word of Heaven.

How great would it be if we could have such an experience every time we listen to a sermon? Unfortunately, even upon hearing the same Word, some experience the work of the Holy Spirit while some simply dismiss it. Young Eun Seo, the author of *I Followed the Yellow Arrow* says that the yellow arrows on the pilgrimage road probably do not hold the same meaning for all pilgrims. For some, those are just signs, but for others, they are like revelations from heaven, the Way, the Truth and the Life.

Christians have professed for a long time that the Bible is the Word of God. However, the Word does not always come upon us in the same way. There are moments when the Word confronts our hearts powerfully. Mark's attic on the day of Pentecost was probably a site of experiencing such a moment. If the Bible is truly inspired by the Holy Spirit, we receive the Word of Heaven as the Spirit pours the Word into our hearts. I pray that God's Word would always come upon our souls in such a manner.

The book that Christian opens in *The Pilgrim's Progress* is the Bible. When he opens the Bible, the Word of Heaven comes alive by the work of the Holy Spirit. He cries out, "What shall I do?" He is finally able to begin his journey to seek the Truth.

Second, we need to face ourselves honestly.

When the Holy Spirit pours the Word of Truth into our hearts, what would our most desperate response look like? When the Holy Spirit's presence is in our heart, He first points out our sin. Remember what Jesus said as He promised to send them the Holy Spirit, the Advocate(companion, comforter):

> "But very truly I tell you, it is for your good that I am going away. Unless I go away, the Advocate will not come to you; but if I go, I will send him to you. When he comes, he will prove the world to be in the wrong about sin and righteousness and judgment"(John 16:7-8).

Therefore, the very first work that the Holy Spirit does when we come into His presence is always self-confrontation. It is to face the reality of our sinfulness that exists deep down in our being. Eventually, we begin to lament just like the Christians in Mark's attic on the day of Pentecost, who cry out, "What shall I do?" just as Christian does in *The Pilgrim's Progress*. A person who has not faced their own sin cannot be called a seeker nor a Christian because that confrontation is the beginning of a seeker's journey.

Recall the moment when the pilgrim of *The Pilgrim's Progress* begins his journey. He is carrying a heavy burden on his back and a book in his hand. He cries out and asks, "What shall I do!"

The Heavenly Word that he reads is like a mirror of his existence. The man wearing ragged clothes in the mirror is an honest reflection of who he is. As a result, he has a heavy burden weighing on his back. Trembling with the guilt of his sin, the seeker finally confronted his true self.

> "Do not merely listen to the word, and so deceive yourselves. Do what it says. Anyone who listens to the word but does not do what it says is like someone who looks at his face in a mirror" (James 1:22-23).

Have you ever stood before the mirror of the Word of Truth? In 2014, I had an opportunity to visit Christian historical sites in England with some of my church members for 10 days. We decided to spend one full day in Bedfordshire, John Bunyan's hometown, and the suburbs of Elstow. We first visited the church and museum that used to be a storage space where Bunyan had meetings and preached the gospel. At the entrance of this church is written,

"The church started in 1650, and the current building was built in 1894." As we walked inside, eight scenes from *The Pilgrim's Progress* were recreated into stained glass work.

One of the eight scenes shows Bunyan writing *The Pilgrim's Progress* in jail, and the next scene portrays Christian the pilgrim with a book in his hand and a burden on his back, listening to Evangelist's instruction. The first sculpture in the Pilgrim's Progress Pilgrimage Park at Pilgrim House in Gapyeong is that of Christian carrying a burden with much anguish. Our journey as seekers begins as we face the reality of sin.

Third, we should not be afraid of paying the price.
Christian, the protagonist of *The Pilgrim's Progress*, shares his anguish with his family. However, his family cannot understand him. They simply assume that he may be mentally unstable. Many seekers experience loneliness as they are misunderstood by those closest to them. Jesus also said, "A man's enemies will be the members of his own household" (Matt. 10:36). He also said, "Whoever does not take up their cross and follow me is not worthy of me" in verse 38.

And so it is. Taking up the cross means completely dying to ourselves. But it is when we die to ourselves that we experience true life and resurrection.

Inevitably, Christian the pilgrim goes on a pilgrimage, the journey of a seeker, on his own. But this doesn't save only himself, but his family as well. His wife and his children, after hearing that Christian reached Celestial City, also start their journey as pilgrims in Part 2 of *The Pilgrim's Progress*. The gift of salvation is not guaranteed for those who avoid paying the price and refuse to take up the cross. One must carry the cross and start the journey.

The writer Young Eun Seo went on her pilgrimage after she wrote her will. She was ready to die when she left. She recounts that she was willing to be "lonely to the point of death" if only she could encounter Jesus. Unexpectedly, she met Jesus waiting for her in the form of a donkey. When a donkey appeared in a green pasture and touched her body with its tender face, she heard a voice resonating in her heart.

"I knew you from long ago."

In that moment, she shouted out, "Oh, God!" and knelt before the donkey with her hands together. She repeatedly said, "Thank you for listening to my prayer. Thank you for encountering me."

She shares that since then, she has never had to ask for a miracle ever again. She was changed. Feeling the presence of Jesus abiding in her was sufficient. The message she heard was: "Do not lean on companions, but walk alone." During her interview after this journey, she talked about what she learned through the pilgrimage.

> "I found love. Love was God's Providence. In His Providence, there is the absolute order of the universe. I was able to understand His love only after I was completely torn apart. After experiencing His love I became a completely different person. That was my salvation."

The crown promised for seekers, who are so desperate for transformation that they are willing to pay the price, is salvation, the love of Christ. She ended her journey on Camino De Santiago with these words:

> "I owe enormously to the many arrows, the sacrifices and commitments of many. I can only pay back by becoming another 'arrow' to direct people who are coming after. This arrow will lead them to the ultimate arrow, the One who said, 'I am the way and the truth and the life. No one comes to the Father(Heaven) except through me.'"

We should also go on our journey as seekers, following the arrows. If you have already encountered Jesus Christ, I pray that you would be another "arrow" that leads others.

Questions for the Pilgrimage of Faith

1. What are the three preparations that we need to have in order to be an earnest seeker?

1)

2)

3)

2. Out of the three, which do you need the most today and why?

3. Have you ever experienced the Word striking your heart and causing you to cry out like Christian in *The Pilgrim's Progress*? Which passage in the Bible led you to the path of a seeker?

4. Are you avoiding any sin that you may need to face? Please confront yourself honestly and determine to die to yourself. Pray that God would give you this kind of courage.

Matthew 3:7

But when he saw many of the Pharisees and Sadducees coming to where he was baptizing, he said to them: "You brood of vipers! Who warned you to flee from the coming wrath?"

Matthew 7:13-14

Enter through the narrow gate. For wide is the gate and broad is the road that leads to destruction, and many enter through it. But small is the gate and narrow the road that leads to life, and only a few find it.

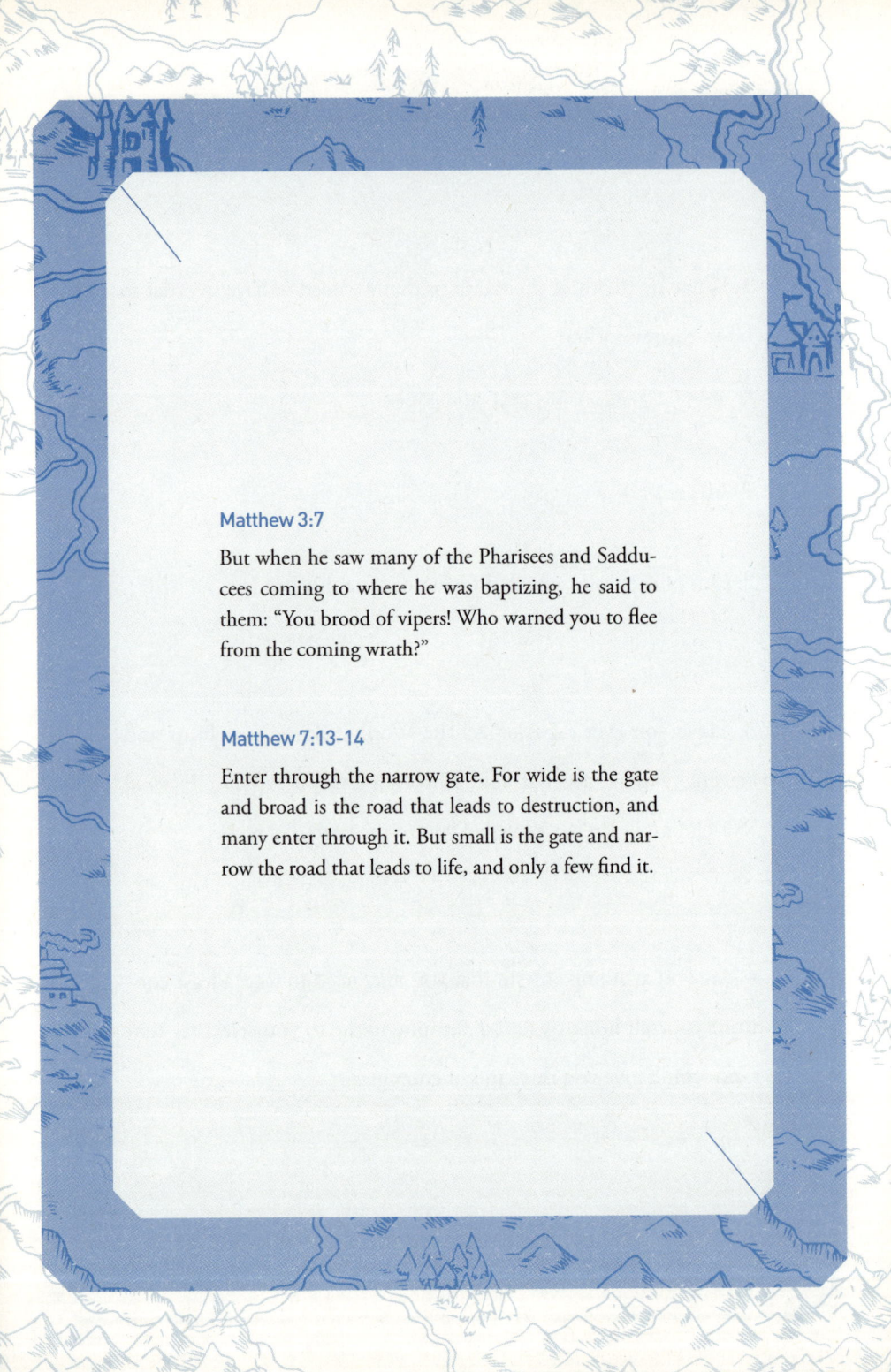

Pilgrim's Progress 5

Evangelist

Evangelist of My Life

All churches emphasize and put much effort into evangelism. If that is the case, what is the first thing that comes to mind when you think of the word "evangelist?" Is it Dr. Billy Graham who preached the Gospel to great crowds in many prominent cities all around the world? Or is it a revival preacher who leads many evangelical revival services at churches across the world? Some might think of Korean street evangelists who shout out "Repent, for the

Kingdom of Heaven is near!" or "Jesus, Heaven! Unbelief, Hell!" at Seoul station or in subway trains. Some people may think of the great layman evangelist gifted with a special talent, leading many souls to Jesus Christ. Who do you think that John Bunyan thought of when he introduced Evangelist in his book?

Scholars who study John Bunyan and his work state that it must have been Pastor John Gifford of Bedford Saint John Church, the church he attended all his life since 1653 (and later pastored at). Unfortunately, the church was not open when I visited. But I saw a sign next to the rectory, on which was written:

"In this House John Bunyan sought spiritual help from John Gifford in the 1650's."

One day John Bunyan was walking in Bedford, praying, and heard a group of women sharing about the assurance of salvation and joy of being born again. He was struck by their conversation. He began to wonder, "Am I really saved? What if it's too late?" He started to read the Bible, and fell into deep spiritual struggle and agony. He then wanted to meet the preacher who planted in the women this assurance of salvation. As soon as he found out that Rev. John Gifford was the pastor of the local church, he requested for a spiritual counseling session.

From that time on, he constantly sought spiritual help from Rev. John Gifford. Rev. Gifford was always available in his rectory to gently answer Bunyan's questions with his Bible open. He became John Bunyan's personal evangelist, just as Jesus was to Nicodemus in John 3 and to the Samaritan woman in chapter 4. Apostle Paul shares about his calling as an evangelist in the following way.

> "He is the one we proclaim, admonishing and teaching everyone with all wisdom, so that we may present everyone fully mature in Christ"(Col. 1:28).

Then, what is the message that evangelists share with their neighbors? We can find the answer by studying an event in *The Pilgrim's Progress*.

What is an Evangelist?

First, an evangelist encourages others to repent before the coming wrath of God.

The moment Christian screams out, "What shall I do?" upon reading the Bible, he is heavily burdened by the concepts of sin and salvation. Finally, just like the jailer in the prison of Philippi, he asks a very specific question as a seeker: "What shall I do to be saved?"

At that moment, Evangelist approaches Christian. Evangelist asks Christian, "Why are you crying out?" Christian answers, "Sir, I read in the book in my hand, that I am condemned to die, and after that to come to judgment. I fear that this burden that is upon my back will sink me lower than the grave, and I shall fall into hell." Then Evangelist opens a parchment roll and reads Matthew 3:7 to him. It says, "Flee from the wrath to come." This signifies repentance in the Christian doctrine.

Repentance is *metanoia* in Greek, meaning "change of direction." It implies that the person's current way of life is wrong. Destruction awaits him, for the wages of sin is death, the wrath of God, and hell.

I once led a conference for Japanese ministers in Beppu, Japan. One of the most heated discussion topics was: "In comparison to Korean churches that are so enthusiastic about evangelism, why don't Japanese churches evangelize?" The conclusion of the discussion was as I had expected. Japanese are extremely polite and self-conscious of others, and therefore afraid of appearing rude. After listening to the discussion, I threw a challenge to the ministers at the closing service.

"I see that there are all kinds of hells here in Beppu, such as the mountain hell, the sun hell, the ocean hell, the valley hell(in fact, there are so many sulfur springs in Beppu that they use the name 'hell' to describe such places). Let's say that a drunken man is approaching one of the sulfur hells, staggering. Would we just sit and watch, trying to be 'polite'? Or, even if we might appear rude, would we shout to warn him that he will die if he does not stop?"

This is the message of repentance. Christian in *The Pilgrim's Progress* hears the message of Evangelist, leaves the City of Destruction(this world), and changes the direction of his life toward the Kingdom of God.

Second, an evangelist encourages others to enter through the narrow gate.

After reading the words that Evangelist shares with him, Christian asks, "Which way should I run?" Then Evangelist, pointing at a large field, asks: "Do you see yonder wicket-gate?" Christian answers, "No." Then Evangelist says, "Do you see yonder shining light?" He continues, "Keep that light in your eye, and go up directly thereto; so shalt thou see the gate. After going through the gate can you find the way to Celestial City." The words that Evangelist shows Christian are from Matthew 7:

> "Enter through the narrow gate. For wide is the gate and broad is the road that leads to destruction, and many enter through it. But small is the gate and narrow the road that leads to life, and only a few find it" (Matt. 7:13-14).

The main point of this story is not that it is difficult to enter through the narrow gate and that it is easy to go through the wide gate. The main issue is the fact that few people want to go through the narrow gate because it is difficult to enter, and many choose to go through the wide gate as it is easy to do so. Likewise, the truth might not always be the popular choice. Sometimes, our family, friends, and neighbors might be against the way of truth that we have chosen. But if the road leads to life, then we need to choose it because an evangelist is someone who guides souls to the way of life, to eternal life. As stated, truth may be not accepted by the majority of people.

Why do many refuse to enter through the narrow gate? Probably because doing so requires a different kind of lifestyle than the way we have lived and the way the world thinks. Entering the narrow gate and walking on the narrow road means that we need to live according to the light Evangelist has shown us, the Word of Truth.

> "Your word is a lamp for my feet, a light on my path"(Ps. 119:105).

As we received the Word of Truth, we no longer live according to the practical standard required by the world's sense of morality. Rather, we live according to the principles of the Word, living a life that transcends this era. This is the pathway that leads us to eternal life. This is why the Christian's way is often very lonely. It is a lonely path that sometimes cannot be understood by our family members and neighbors.

Christian in *The Pilgrim's Progress*, who is about to start his journey as a seeker, also faces opposition from his family members. His wife and his children tell him to hurry and come back. His neighbors are either sarcastic with him or threaten him to return. But he has to go through the narrow gate and walk the narrow road as Evangelist has shown him, for this is the path to eternal life.

Jesus, the Public Evangelist.

It is a great blessing to live as an evangelist who leads the lost to eternal life. Jesus, the Son of God, also came to the world for the evangelistic mission.

> "For the Son of Man came to seek and to save the lost" (Luke 19:10).

Think about how Jesus lived out a life of an evangelist on earth. Of course, Jesus lived a life of a public evangelist who professed the gospel to the crowds every time He could. Yet, he also lived a life of a personal evangelist who spent time with individuals to lead them to eternal life. John 3 and 4 are accounts of him as a personal evangelist.

In John 3, a man comes into the scene. Jesus engages in a very long conversation about the gospel with this man. In chapter 4, Jesus spends no insignificant amount of time with a woman at the well to share the Gospel. Jesus shared the gospel with everyone, regardless of their gender.

The man in John 3 is Nicodemus. He was a well respected member of the Sanhedrin. But in chapter 4 a nameless Samaritan woman appears. This woman is socially isolated and ostracized by everyone because of her immoral lifestyle. Jesus proclaims the Gospel to everyone, whether they have power or not. In chapter 3, Nicodemus encounters Jesus at night. In John 4, the Samaritan woman meets Jesus at noon. Jesus is always open to meet people, night and day.

In chapter 3, the male protagonist Nicodemus comes with the intention to meet Jesus. On the other hand, in chapter 4, Jesus arrives at the well first and waits for the Samaritan woman. Jesus shared the gospel not only with people who were ready but also with those who were not.

The conversation that Nicodemus had with Jesus in chapter 3 was on being "born again." Jesus and the Samaritan woman in chapter 4 talk about the "spring of water welling up to eternal life." However, what Jesus did ultimately through all these conversations was to lead people to the path of eternal life. This is the call of an evangelist.

When we meditate on John 4, we often think that the climax of the story is when the Samaritan woman recognizes Jesus as Christ. But her story does not end there. The message that we need to focus on in chapter 4 is as follows:

> "Then, leaving her water jar, the woman went back to the town and said to the people, 'Come, see a man who told me everything I ever did. Could this be the Messiah?' They came out of the town and made their way toward him" (John 4:28-30).

What happened here? The Samaritan woman who was thirsty and sought for eternal living water became an evangelist who led others to the way of life. I hope that every Christian on earth will live a life of an evangelist just like this Samaritan woman.

Questions for the Pilgrimage of Faith

1. What are the two things that an evangelist should encourage?
1)
2)

2. What do you need today to live a life of an evangelist?

3. What do you think is the mission of an evangelist?

4. Rev. John Gifford was a personal evangelist to John Bunyan. Do you have an evangelist figure to whom you can ask for spiritual help? Also, are you an evangelist who provides spiritual help to others?

Matthew 13:1-9

That same day Jesus went out of the house and sat by the lake. Such large crowds gathered around him that he got into a boat and sat in it, while all the people stood on the shore. Then he told them many things in parables, saying: "A farmer went out to sow his seed. As he was scattering the seed, some fell along the path, and the birds came and ate it up. Some fell on rocky places, where it did not have much soil. It sprang up quickly, because the soil was shallow. But when the sun came up, the plants were scorched, and they withered because they had no root. Other seed fell among thorns, which grew up and choked the plants. Still other seed fell on good soil, where it produced a crop—a hundred, sixty or thirty times what was sown. Whoever has ears, let them hear."

Pilgrim's Progress 6

Types of Seekers

The Singing Evangelist

There was a young man named Knowles Shaw who was born to a poor farmer in Ohio, USA, in the mid-1800s. He was naturally talented in music and taught himself how to play the violin. At the age of 12, he lost his father. He had to take over the family business to support his mother and siblings. Early in the morning he went out to the field to sow seeds. But because he could not support his family with farming alone, he visited parties and played the violin as a side job. Playing the violin at parties was more profitable than farming.

This young head of the household grew up and turned 20 years old. As usual, he was playing his violin at a party, entertaining people. All of sudden, he was reminded of his father who passed away, and it was as if he could hear his father's voice. "Son, prepare yourself to meet God. I want your voice and your instrument to be used for God."

After the party, Shaw went home crying and immediately went to church where he was baptized. Many years later, he became a "singing evangelist" who played the violin and preached God's word. Throughout his lifetime, he baptised over 20,000 people. The most representative among the hymns that he wrote lyrics for is "Bringing in the Sheaves" (New Hymnal 496).

> "Sowing in the morning, sowing seeds of kindness,
> Sowing in the noontide and the dewy eve;
> Waiting for the harvest, and the time of reaping,
> We shall come rejoicing, bringing in the sheaves."

The second verse of this hymn tells us, "Sowing in the sunshine, sowing in the shadows; Fearing neither clouds nor winter's chilling breeze; By and by, the harvest and the labor ended; We shall come rejoicing, bringing in the sheaves." The third verse goes: "Going forth with weeping, sowing for the Master; Tho', the loss sustained, our spirit often grieves; when our weeping's over; He will bid us welcome; we shall come rejoicing, bringing in the sheaves." Likewise, today's Christians should go out to the world with the gospel and sow seeds of the Word.

As we plant seeds of the gospel, we face many different types of seekers. In the parable of the sower, Jesus talks about four different types of seekers that we will face as we sow the Word. John Bunyan also presents the different types of seekers in *The Pilgrim's Progress*.

Four Different Types of Seekers

First, there are seekers like the "path."

When Jesus spoke about the parable of the sower, He probably was referring to the path between fields in Palestine. There were well-paved roads due to Roman influence, but most of the roads in Palestine were pathways in between fields. Farmers, townsmen, and travelers usually walked on these roads. As they frequently passed through these paths, the roads became hardened and had a smooth surface. This is where the seeds fell. But what happened as soon as they fell?

> "As he was scattering the seed, some fell along the path, and the birds came and ate it up"(Matt. 13:4).

Later, Jesus interprets this passage for the disciples.

> "When anyone hears the message about the kingdom and does not understand it, the evil one comes and snatches away what was sown in their heart. This is the seed sown along the path"(Matt. 13:19).

The path symbolizes a man whose heart is already hardened and therefore cannot absorb the Word. Because the devil soon snatches away the Word, he cannot bear fruit. We should expect to encounter such people when we evangelize.

One of those who follow Christian as he leaves the City of Destruction in *The Pilgrim's Progress* is Obstinate. He asks Christian why he is leaving his hometown. Christian answers, "I seek a place that can never be destroyed, one that is pure, and that fadeth not away, and it is laid up in heaven, and safe there, to be given, at the time appointed, to them that seek it with all their heart. Read it so, if you will, in my book."

However, Obstinate in the end refuses Christian's words and returns to the City of Destruction because his heart is like the path. His heart is hardened by his stubbornness, closed shut against the Word of God.

To such people, even if the Word is preached to them many times, the devil snatches it away so that their hearts cannot absorb it. We often encounter these kinds of people when we evangelize. Nevertheless, they are still seekers that ask us questions and sometimes try to persuade us with their own opinions.

Second, there are seekers like the "rocky places."

If we visit Israel, we can see that there are many rocky fields. Especially because there is a lot of limestone, the seeds sown in those places cannot put down roots and end up dying quickly.

> "Some fell on rocky places, where it did not have much soil. It sprang up quickly, because the soil was shallow. But when the sun came up, the plants were scorched, and they withered because they had no root" (Matt. 13:5-6).

What kind of seeker do these rocky places represent? Listen to

Jesus' interpretation.

> "The seed falling on rocky ground refers to someone who hears the word and at once receives it with joy. But since they have no root, they last only a short time. When trouble or persecution comes because of the word, they quickly fall away" (Matt. 13:20-21).

Seekers that are like rocky places temporarily agree with the Word preached to them and even cry and rejoice with the Word, but they soon vanish from the gathering of the faithful. They say that faith does not benefit them but rather causes inconvenience and loss. They cannot bear even small trials and persecutions, so they forfeit their faith and disappear like the wind.

Pliable who is presented with Obstinate in *The Pilgrim's Progress* is an example. Pliable turns down Obstinate's offer to return together to the City of Destruction. He agrees with the words of Christian and says, "I intend to go along with this good man, and to cast in my lot with him." He follows Christian. Unfortunately, his journey with Christian does not last long. As they walk mindlessly, they fall into the Slough of Despond in the center of an open field. Pliable barely escapes the swamp and yells at Christian, "Is this the happiness you have told me all this while of?" He shouts and turns away at once and disappears. Just like his name, his journey as a seeker ends in another whim.

We come across a good number of people who are just like Pliable, who break away from the road of faith. This parable exhorts us to stay on the path, unwavering, despite the whims of so many people who pass us by. Caprice is not a virtue but a vice.

Third, there are seekers like the "thorny fields."
Seeds that fall on thorny fields are pitiful as they appear to sprout for a little, but soon are choked by thorns and therefore cannot bear fruit. Jesus warns the third type of seekers who fail to bear fruit due to their worldly desires.

> "Other seed fell among thorns, which grew up and choked the plants" (Matt. 13:7).

Let's take a look at Jesus' interpretation of the seekers whose hearts are like thorny fields.

> "The seed falling among the thorns refers to someone who hears the word, but the worries of this life and the deceitfulness of wealth choke the word, making it unfruitful" (Matt. 13:22).

It is not that they do not have any interest in the Word. They have cravings for the Word and listen to the Word because they are fairly passionate about it. But they have a bigger interest, a bigger greed: a worldly desire for wealth.

There was a rich ruler who came to see Jesus. He was interested in eternal life and was desperately seeking the truth. But in the end he left, turning his back on Jesus because of his greed for wealth and anxiety over losing worldly treasures. This is the life of a seeker with a heart full of thorns.

In *The Pilgrim's Progress*, there is a character just like the rich ruler. Christian and Hopeful come in contact with Demas on their pilgrimage. Demas tempts them to stop by the Silver Mine. Who is Demas? Listen to Apostle Paul's account.

> "For Demas, because he loved this world, has deserted me and has gone to Thessalonica" (2 Tim. 4:10).

Even today, how many pilgrims end up deserting the seeker's path because they cannot overcome the temptation of the Silver Mine? The reason that there are more and more of them is that they cannot differentiate between God and gold. Gold is only one letter away from God. Does "gold" look like God to you? If so, watch out. You may be on Demas' path.

Fourth, there are seekers like the "good soil."
Just as it is written in the hymn by Knowles Shaw, we do not need to worry if the seeds that we sow do not sprout. This is because we will certainly meet good soil that God has prepared beforehand.

> "Still other seed fell on good soil, where it produced a crop—a hundred, sixty or thirty times what was sown" (Matt. 13:8).

We can find Jesus' interpretation about the good soil also in Luke's account.

> "But the seed on good soil stands for those with a noble and good heart, who hear the word, retain it, and by persevering produce a crop" (Luke 8:15).

In this verse, Luke emphasizes that seekers who are like the good soil not only hear and respond to the Word, but also hold on to the Word and endure.

Christian in *The Pilgrim's Progress* is a seeker like the good soil. Even though he falls into the Slough of Despond with Pliable, he does not give up on seeking the truth. Right at that moment, Help comes and reaches out his hand to rescue Christian from the swamp. He tells Christian to carefully continue to walk towards the narrow gate. By enduring hardship and experiencing the help of God, he proves himself to be a true pilgrim. Through this experience, Christian becomes a stronger pilgrim who can now ask others to join his journey of life and salvation.

Many missionaries in China had to leave the country during the Cultural Revolution. One missionary asked a pastor who was discipled under him and had become a faithful church leader in China, "Are you ready to endure the anticipated hardships?" The pastor replied, "Missionary, there is hot water and a tea bag here. I put the tea bag into the hot water. Does the flavor of the tea dissolve completely? No. Rather, the true flavor of the tea is infused within the hot water. Likewise, the trials of the Chinese Church are an opportunity for true believers to prove their faith is genuine. Please pray for us."

In fact, this time of persecution turned out to be a great opportunity that refined the Chinese Christians' faith.

Even when difficult times come, I hope that we can take our hardships as opportunities to prove that we are seekers like the good soil.

Evangelist Knowles Shaw who sang that we shall be "sowing in the morning and the dewy eves" died young at the age of 44 from a train accident. Before taking his last breath he confessed, "It is a grand thing to rally people to the cross of Christ." I pray that we all can experience the sincerity of this confession.

Questions for the Pilgrimage of Faith

1. Explain the four types of seekers.

1)

2)

3)

4)

2. What is important in order to become a seeker like the good soil?

3. What kind of a seeker are you right now?

4. What can you do in order to abandon obstinacy, whims and greed, and to not give up on truth-seeking?

Even when difficult times come,
I hope that we can take our hardships
as opportunities to prove
that we are seekers like the good soil.

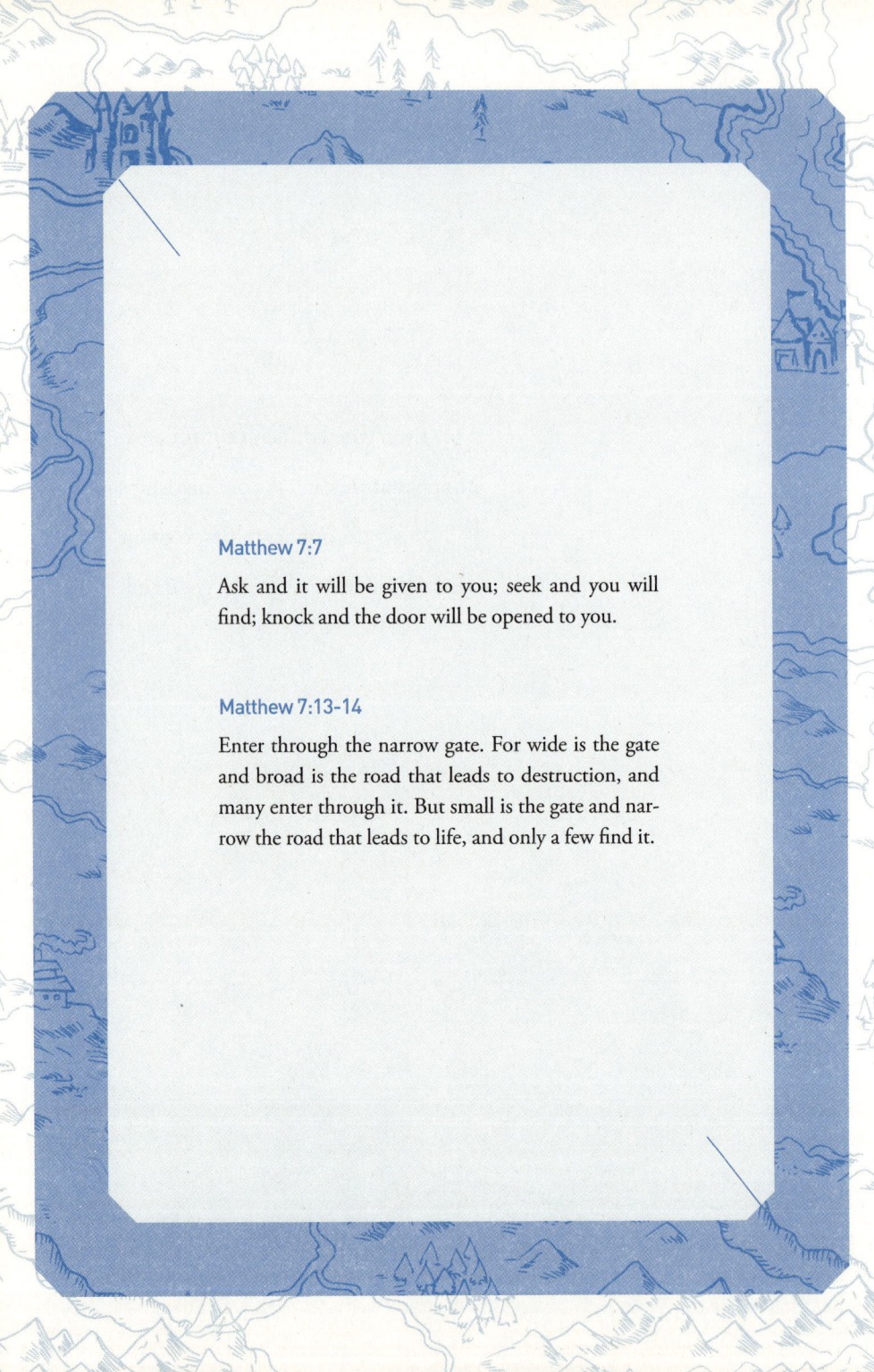

Matthew 7:7

Ask and it will be given to you; seek and you will find; knock and the door will be opened to you.

Matthew 7:13-14

Enter through the narrow gate. For wide is the gate and broad is the road that leads to destruction, and many enter through it. But small is the gate and narrow the road that leads to life, and only a few find it.

Pilgrim's Progress 7

The Wicket Gate

Is The Majority Always Right?

The best political system that modern humanity has discovered is perhaps democracy. Living in the post-modern generation, we have naturally accepted that "the view of the majority is always right." But think about Nicolaus Copernicus' heliocentric theory. Until he came up with this theory, the majority of mankind believed that Earth was flat and that if you went to the end, you would fall off a cliff. They believed without a doubt that all celestial bodies revolved around Earth. How about now? The theory that the majority held onto has been proven wrong. It is now revealed that Earth is round and that it revolves around the sun.

Having experienced that even the majority's judgment can have errors like this, mankind concluded that a true spirit of democracy would take into account both the majority judgment and the minority opinion, following a process of negotiation, debate, and research. The Bible gives a word of caution about the majority's conclusion:

> "Do not follow the crowd in doing wrong. When you give testimony in a lawsuit, do not pervert justice by siding with the crowd" (Ex. 23:3).

More than anything else, the Bible warns us against following the majority on the way to salvation. That is the wide gate, the broad road. In Matthew 7:13, the wide gate is described as "the gate that leads to destruction." And the Bible teaches that the road that the gate leads to is the "road of destruction." Jesus warns that there will be many (the majority) who choose to walk that road. On the other hand, the narrow gate "leads to life," and though the road may be narrow it is the "way of salvation." But those who choose that road will be few (the minority). When it comes to salvation, the majority's choice may not be the truth.

Then what does the Bible specifically mean by choosing between the wide gate and the narrow gate, the broad road and the narrow road? We can find a clear and excellent answer from *The Pilgrim's Progress*.

The Difference Between the Wide Gate and the Narrow Gate

First, the wide gate and the broad road refers to living according to the law.
Not long after Christian receives help in the Slough of Despond, he encounters a new character, Mr. Worldly Wiseman. He asks Christian, "How now, good fellow! Whither away after this burdened manner?" Christian replies, "I am going to the small sheep gate that lies ahead, following Evangelist's directions." Mr. Worldly Wiseman offers to show Christian an easy road to lay down his burden and points to a village called Morality. He should meet Mr. Legality when he reaches the town, and the man will take Christian's burden away. Mr. Worldly Wiseman kindly adds that if the man is not home, he can meet with his son, Civility.

This symbolizes the way of salvation that Mr. Worldly Wiseman points to. Anyone who keeps the law and is civil can be saved. In fact, don't most people on this earth think the same? The wide gate and the broad road is the common way people pursue salvation by keeping the law, morality, or courtesy.

This is why Christian is surrounded by fear when he sees lightning, thunder, and fire arise from the mountains above as he climbs the hill. His burden feels heavier, and he breaks out in a cold sweat. The mountain he climbs with much difficulty is Mount Sinai, where Moses received the law.

What is the law? The law consists of "do's" and "don'ts." We often think that if we do what God or our conscience commands us to do and don't do what we should not do, we will be made righteous and be saved. However, where does this law lead us to? This is where John Bunyan introduces Galatians 3:10.

> "For all who rely on the works of the law are under a curse, as it is written: 'Cursed is everyone who does not continue to do everything written in the Book of the Law.'"

The characteristic of the law is that it is not satisfied with our best. Even if we were to keep the law but miss one single command, we would be deemed sinners unable to escape from God's judgment and curse. This is why no one can earn righteousness before God by keeping the law. The law is God's holy principle that gives us moral standards, but despite its purpose, it leads us to the cursed road.

There is a book that talks about this attribute of the law through an interesting parable. It is *God Without Religion* by Andrew Farley, and in the book the author depicts the law as a "spouse that does not know satisfaction."

David and Shelly have been married for the past 9 years. In the first few years, David felt like he was in heaven as he was filled with the joy of having the perfect wife. However, his perfectionist wife saw areas to "work on" in her husband David and started making a list of things he needed to fix. She designed the perfect plan that would transform him, and she required him each day to do what she wanted him to do. When he couldn't show changes in his life, the wife finally warned him of divorce. She complained about her spouse's lazy habits and low income.

"Look at other men. They have clear life goals and their life is stable. How long are you going to live such an unstable life?"

He was determined to do his best in order to satisfy his wife. He worked as a construction site director during the week, and on weekends he worked as a car salesman to earn more income. But he couldn't meet his wife's high demands. He always shrank before her and lived with a sense of shame and guilt that he could never meet her standards. In the end, his wife handed him the divorce papers.

The author says that anyone under the law is like the man who married a perfectionist spouse. He is always anxious and afraid that he might get divorced. Those who say, "I don't believe in Jesus but I live according to my conscience," also live as those under the law of conscience. If they cannot live according to what their conscience requires, where will their salvation be? This is the reason that the law or conscience and courtesy cannot be the way of salvation. We learn here that if we follow worldly wisdom, we will be led to destruction.

Second, the narrow gate and the narrow road is living by faith.
After losing his way from Worldly Wiseman's deceit, Christian is brought to his senses thanks to Evangelist's intervention. As Evangelist exhorts Christian to head to the Wicket Gate again he shares the following verses:

> "But my righteous one will live by faith. And I take no pleasure in the one who shrinks back"(Heb. 10:38).

> "But we do not belong to those who shrink back and are destroyed, but to those who have faith and are saved"(Heb. 10:39).

Salvation is not earned by the act of keeping the law, but depends on accepting the gift of God in faith. Therefore, the Wicket Gate and narrow road lead us to the road of faith. With a word of caution and encouragement from Evangelist, Christian hastens towards the Wicket Gate again. After walking a distance, Christian at last reaches the Wicket Gate. On the doorpost of the Wicket Gate is written Matthew 7:7:

> "Ask and it will be given to you; seek and you will find; knock and the door will be opened to you."

Salvation does not depend on what we do but it is rather a gift from God. But this salvation is a heavenly gift prepared for those who seek the way of salvation and knock on its door, for the act of knocking is a demonstration of faith.

> "For it is by grace you have been saved, through faith—and this is not from yourselves, it is the gift of God" (Eph. 2:8).

As Christian hesitantly knocks on the Wicket Gate, Goodwill opens the door and asks, "Who is there?" Christian replies, "Here is a poor burdened sinner. I come from the City of Destruction, but am going to Mount Zion, that I may be set free from the wrath to come; I would therefore, sir, since I am told that by this gate is the way thither, know, if you are willing to let me in." Then Goodwill welcomes Christian with all his heart and shares John 6:37:

> "All those the Father gives me will come to me, and whoever comes to me I will never drive away."

Then he pulls Christian inside the door.

"A little distance from this gate there is erected a strong castle, of which Beelzebub, the Evil One, is the captain; from whence both he and they that are with him shoot arrows at those that come up to this gate, if haply they may die before they can enter in. But don't worry. Follow the narrow but straight way you see ahead of you. This is the way our patriarchs paved out for us."

What does this mean? Satan incessantly keeps us from going

through the Wicket Gate and walking the narrow road because it is the road to salvation, to life, and to eternity. This parable shows that there are two different ways in which people seek salvation: the wide gate and the narrow gate, and the broad road and the narrow road. One leads to destruction, and the other leads to life.

> "Enter through the narrow gate. For wide is the gate and broad is the road that leads to destruction, and many enter through it. But small is the gate and narrow the road that leads to life, and only a few find it" (Matt. 7:13-14).

The Way of the Law vs. The Way of Faith

As shown in *The Pilgrim's Progress*, the broad road is the way of the law that Mr. Worldly Wiseman teaches and the narrow road is the way of faith that the Evangelist teaches. The law tells us that there might be salvation if we live according to the law and our conscience by our own strength. Faith tells us that there is sure salvation only if we receive grace as a gift that God has already fulfilled.

Law tells us to "do," but faith tells us that it is "done." Law leads us to Mount Sinai, but faith leads us to Calvary. Salvation by law depends on the self whereas salvation by faith is already achieved by the Savior. Law binds us, but faith frees us. This is why Christianity is not a religion but rather Good News.

Are you joyfully walking the narrow road, having heard the gospel, encountering Jesus and enjoying the grace of salvation? Or are you walking and sweating on the broad road of morality paved to Mount Sinai, carrying the burden of the law to please God with your own works?

If you are at the wide gate and the broad road, promptly make a turn and come to the narrow gate of salvation made ready by God. Do not hesitate. Knock and ask God to save you. You are not asking for the sake of your works, but for the sake of His mercy and compassion in faith. Depend only on the grace that comes from God sending His Son Jesus as the Savior to save us, and receive the salvation He accomplished through the cross of Jesus. Look at this promise in Romans 10:9-10.

> "If you declare with your mouth, 'Jesus is Lord,' and believe in your heart that God raised him from the dead, you will be saved. For it is with your heart that you believe and are justified, and it is with your mouth that you profess your faith and are saved."

Now is the time to confess that Jesus Christ, God's Son who came down to Earth, is our Lord and Savior instead of relying on our worthless works as the foundation of our salvation. This is how we knock on the door of salvation. At this moment the door of salvation opens and we become pilgrims who walk the road of life, of eternity, and of salvation. I am not walking alone but with the help of those God has prepared for me such as Evangelist and Goodwill. This road of pilgrimage is narrow, but holy and beautiful. If you have not yet knocked on the door, do so right now in faith.

Questions for the Pilgrimage of Faith

1. Explain the difference between the wide gate and the narrow gate.

2. What law keeps binding us and leading us to the wide road?

3. What do we need to do to enter the narrow gate?

4. What does it mean to knock on the narrow gate in faith?

Salvation is not earned by the act of keeping the law, but depends on accepting the gift of God in faith. Therefore, the Wicket Gate and narrow road lead us to the road of faith.

Luke 23:33-34

When they came to the place called the Skull, they crucified him there, along with the criminals—one on his right, the other on his left. Jesus said, "Father, forgive them, for they do not know what they are doing." And they divided up his clothes by casting lots.

Luke 23:42-43

Then he said, "Jesus, remember me when you come into your kingdom." Jesus answered him, "Truly I tell you, today you will be with me in paradise."

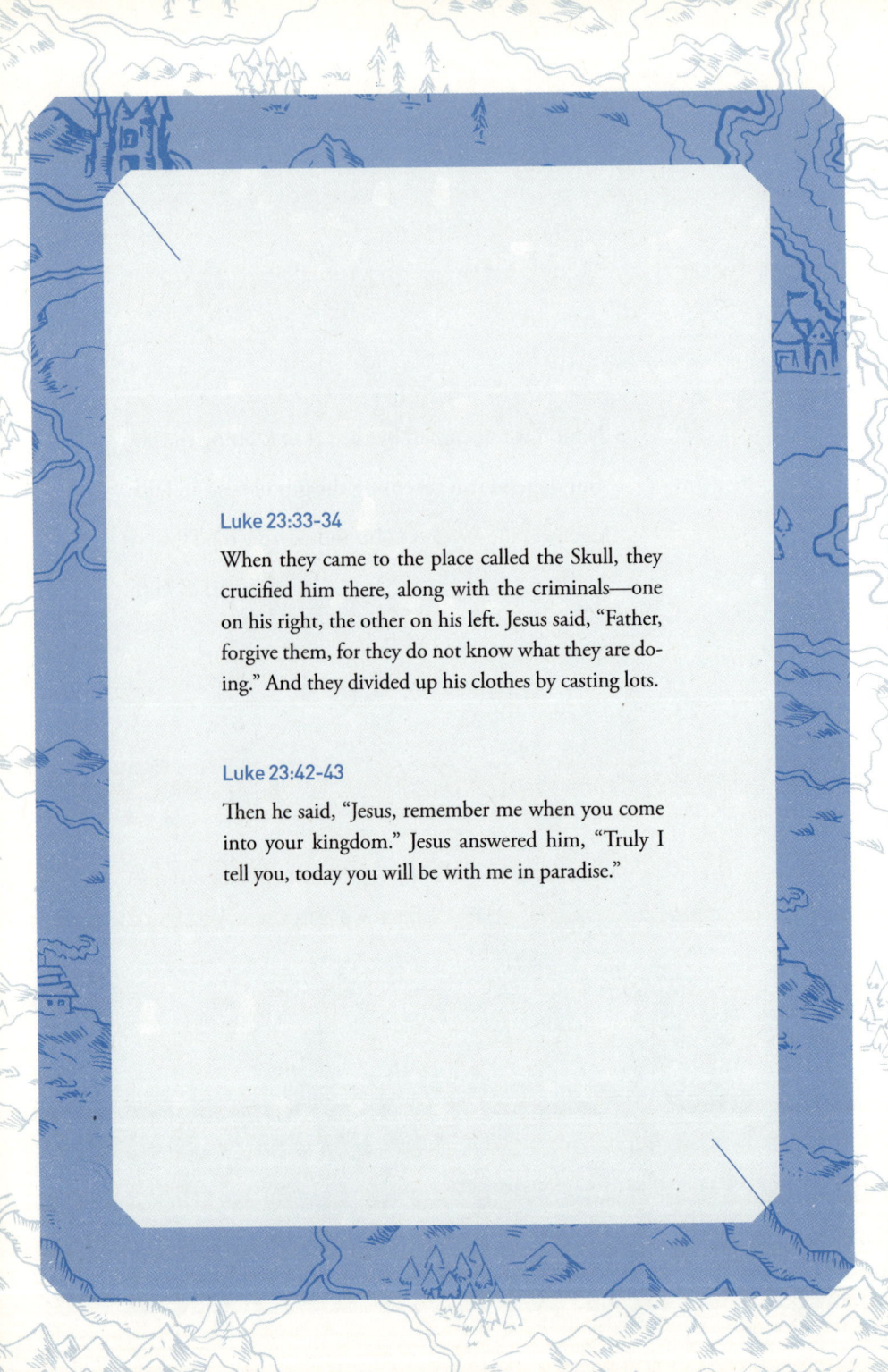

Pilgrim's Progress 8

The Hill of the Cross

The Real Meaning of Freedom

In our nation's history, we have experienced gaining freedom from Japanese colonial rule. Is there a symbolic image that comes to mind when you talk about freedom? Many people would think of the Statue of Liberty. It was a gift from France to celebrate the 100th year of independence for the United States. In her right hand, the statue is holding a torch, which is a symbol of peace, and the U.S. Declaration of Independence in the other. On the cornerstone is written, "Give me your tired, your poor, your huddled masses yearning to breathe free." The seven cutting edges in the crown on her head symbolize freedom spreading out to the seven seas of the world. This is why the statue's official name is "Liberty Enlightening the World."

In the movie *The Admiral: Roaring Currents*, which once was very popular in Korea, Admiral Sun Sin Yi says, "To abandon the sea is to abandon Chosun." The sea was like the doorway to Chosun and at the same time a symbol of freedom to go out to the world. To abandon it would mean to lose freedom and be imprisoned in this land. In the same way, it would not be a stretch to identify the history of mankind as a pursuit of freedom and its enjoyment. Yet, have we really found freedom to the extent of enjoying it?

Where can we find the true meaning of freedom? The answer is not at the Statue of Liberty but at the hill of Calvary, the hill of the cross. *The Pilgrim's Progress* shows most vibrantly how mankind's real freedom was proclaimed there. After passing through the Wicket Gate, Christian's heavy burden comes loose the moment he reaches the hill of the cross. For the first time, his burden of sin is taken away, and he tastes real freedom. Beyond political freedom, this was spiritual freedom.

As Christian stands before the cross, three angels appear to him.

What the three angels do is the essence of the spiritual freedom we need to experience.

The Three Shining Ones that Christian Encounters

The First Angel: Declaration of Forgiveness of Sins

Look at how John Bunyan describes Christian when he arrives at the hill of the cross:

> "He ran thus till he came to a place somewhat ascending; and upon that place stood a Cross, and a little below, in the bottom, a tomb. So I saw in my dream, that just as Christian came up with the cross, his burden loosed from off his shoulders, and fell from off his back, and began to tumble, and so continued to do till it came to the mouth of the tomb, where it fell in, and I saw it no more. Then was Christian glad and lightsome, and said with a merry heart, 'He hath given me rest by His sorrow, and life by His death.' Then he stood still awhile to look and wonder; for it was very surprising to him that the sight of the cross should thus ease him of his burden. He looked, therefore, and looked again, even till the springs that

were in his head sent the water down his cheeks."

At that moment, the first angel comes near and proclaims, "Your sins are forgiven." John Bunyan then references Mark 2:5. It is the scene in which Jesus tells the paralyzed man, "Your sins are forgiven." In the following verses the teachers of the law start saying that Jesus blasphemed. They say that no one except for God can dare forgive sins. Their questions and complaints were not wrong, but there was a truth that they did not know. That Jesus was God.

As God Himself, Jesus proclaimed forgiveness of sins. The Bible diagnoses that sin is the most important existential crisis that mankind faces. We have all sinned and as a result, we live as slaves to sin.

> Jesus replies, "Very truly I tell you, everyone who sins is a slave to sin" (John 8:34).

The greatest fear that rules over man's unconscious is the guilt complex. *Crime and Punishment* by Dostoyevski might be the literary work that portrayed this truth most accurately. Raskolnikov, the protagonist, is an atheist who adheres to western rationalism. He murders an elderly pawnbroker. He thinks that it would be beneficial for everyone if someone who does more harm than good would simply not exist. However, what he considers to be his just belief is soon wavered by a sense of guilt, and when Sonya the sacred prostitute suggests to him to repent, he finally turns himself in and leaves to Siberia. Sonya here was used as God's instrument. Through her, the protagonist admits and confesses his sin, and is released from guilt to live a free life. The forgiveness of sins becomes the new starting point of his life.

The Second Angel: Putting On of New Garments

The second angel who appears before Christian as he reaches the mount strips him of his dirty clothes and puts new clothes on him. In this part John Bunyan quotes from Zechariah 3.

> "The angel said to those who were standing before him, 'Take off his filthy clothes.' Then he said to Joshua, 'See, I have taken away your sin, and I will put fine garments on you'" (Zech. 3:4).

This is the work of grace that takes us a step beyond the initial grace that forgives sins. This reminds us of the incident when the father takes off the prodigal son's clothes and gives him new and beautiful garments. Apostle Paul says that this is like putting off the old self and putting on the new self (Eph. 4:22-24).

Clothing is an indication of our status. Think about a military uniform, police uniform, or judicial ermine. Don't these attires make the soldiers, police officers, and judges act in a way worthy of their clothing? The fact that the pilgrim had been wearing filthy clothes indicates that he had the status of a sinner. However, the moment we accept Jesus Christ, who died on the cross for us and was raised to life three days later, we are not only forgiven by the blood that he shed but also receive justification as Paul testifies.

> "And all are justified freely by his grace through the redemption that came by Christ Jesus" (Rom. 3:24).

"Justification" does not mean that we become righteous, but that we are declared righteous. It means that there has been a change in our status. We were sinners but we are now righteous ones. Of course, the transformation into a life worthy of the status is also an important process that must follow. Yet, without a change of status there is no change of life. When a president is elected, from that moment he is given the status of a president-elect as well as the respect fit for that status. It might feel awkward in the beginning even for the president himself, but as that person becomes increasingly conscious of their new status over time, actions respective to the status become natural. This is why God first gives us the status and then asks us for a transformed life that fits it. Think about how confident Christian must have felt when he took off his dirty clothes and put on new beautiful garments. He would never be able to forget the overwhelming moment he started a new life of true freedom.

The Third Angel: Sealing and the Gift of the Scroll

In *The Pilgrim's Progress*, the third angel approaches Christian and puts a seal on his forehead. In this part John Bunyan quotes from Ephesians 1.

> "And you also were included in Christ when you heard the message of truth, the gospel of your salvation. When you believed, you were marked in him with a seal, the promised Holy Spirit" (Eph. 1:13).

What does sealing mean? It means a sense of belonging, or sovereignty. Now it is clear who the master is. The one who seals has to take responsibility of the one sealed. By hearing the gospel and believing in Jesus Christ, Christian is sealed as one belonging to Christ and as a child of God. This was the work of the Holy Spirit.

In Ephesians 1, Apostle Paul describes the identity of the saints in Christ by explaining it through the work of the Trinity: the Father, the Son, and the Holy Spirit. God the Father chooses, the Son redeems, and the Holy Spirit seals. Maybe John Bunyan also wanted to describe the hill of the cross in the same way. This is why biblical scholar Warren Wiersbe also says that the three angels describe the work of salvation by the Trinity. God the Father proclaims forgiveness of sins, the Son puts on the garments of righteousness, and the Holy Spirit seals.

However, the third angel's work does not end with sealing. After he marks Christian's forehead, he hands him a scroll with a seal on it. He tells Christian to open it often as he goes his way. He tells him that he will need it until the day he reaches New Jerusalem. What does the scroll mean? Without a doubt it is the Bible, the Word of God. Written on scrolls in the past, the Bible itself is God's Word written by the inspiration of the Holy Spirit.

> "Above all, you must understand that no prophecy of Scripture came about by the prophet's own interpretation of things. For prophecy never had its origin in the human will, but prophets, though human, spoke from God as they were carried along by the Holy Spirit" (2 Pet. 1:20-21).

2 Timothy says the following about the role of the Scripture:

> "All Scripture is God-breathed and is useful for teaching, rebuking, correcting and training in righteousness" (2 Tim. 3:16).

What should those who have been set free by the gospel at the cross do now? They should not be walking the road of faith in whichever way pleases them, but rather, by holding onto the Word of God, walk according to the Word's guidance. Let's give our ears to the psalmist's confession.

> "Oh, how I love your law! I meditate on it all day long" (Ps. 119:97).

> "Your word is a lamp for my feet, a light on my path" (Ps. 119:105).

This is the secret to how we can walk this road while guarding the spiritual freedom we have.

Guarding Spiritual Freedom

It has been 70 years since our nation gained independence from Japan. It is by God's amazing grace that Korea gained precious freedom from Japanese colonial rule. However, we should no longer look at why we lost this freedom in political terms, but as a moral and spiritual problem. Guarding the spiritual freedom of being right with God and the moral freedom of having a clean conscience is far more important and fundamental than keeping political freedom. God's Word is our weapon that helps us guard this spiritual and moral freedom.

Once there was a memorial event organized to remember the release of Jews from the Auschwitz concentration camp in Poland. One of the former prisoners reminisced, "There should never have been a hell like Auschwitz. To prevent repeating hell, we must not forget Auschwitz. We must not forget that our mistake made a hell on earth. And now we all must promise that we will never make one ever again."

But we are weak, and a man-made promise cannot guard our freedom.

The Bible tells us that God made man in His image and that Jesus came down and died on the cross to restore His image in us. We are saved because we have invited Jesus, the Son of God, into our hearts. To guard the dignified freedom given to us, we need to hold onto the Word of God. We can walk towards heaven and not towards hell only if we hold fast to the Word that the third angel has given us.

Questions for the Pilgrimage of Faith

1. Summarize the experiences that Christian of *The Pilgrim's Progress* has with the three angels he encounters on the Hill of the Cross.
1) The first angel:
2) The second angel:
3) The third angel:

2. What does Christian need in order to continue guarding his freedom?

3. What did John Bunyan hope to portray through the three angels in *The Pilgrim's Progress*?

4. Have you encountered the three angels and are you experiencing true spiritual freedom?

1 Corinthians 3:1

Brothers and sisters, I could not address you as people who live by the Spirit but as people who are still worldly—mere infants in Christ.

1 Corinthians 4:15

Even if you had ten thousand guardians in Christ, you do not have many fathers, for in Christ Jesus I became your father through the gospel.

Pilgrim's Progress 9

The Interpreter

The Road to Spiritual Maturity

In 2014, Korea was bustling because of the visit of Pope Francis(Jorge Mario Bergoglio). Indeed, we were able to experience the remarkable impact that an esteemed spiritual leader could have. In Catholicism, the Pope or a priest is called "Papa"("priest" officially) as a name of endearment. But as we read the Bible, we find out that the presence of a spiritual father is not simply determined by the physical church's office. The term spiritual father refers to all those who give birth to spiritual children and raise them up. The moment we believe in Jesus Christ as our Lord and Savior, we receive Christ's new life as a gift and are born in Him as spiritual babies.

> "Brothers and sisters, I could not address you as people who live by the Spirit but as people who are still worldly—mere infants in Christ"(1 Cor. 3:1).

There were many spiritual children in the Corinthian church(around AD 52) planted by Apostle Paul. However, they were not maturing into godly Christians. 2 Corinthians is the letter that Apostle Paul wrote(around AD 54-55) from Ephesus in order to urge spiritual maturity in the Corinthian church.

Christians' lifelong task is simply put as walking the road of spiritual maturity. If there is a blessing we all need to experience at a certain level of maturity, it would be to live as spiritual fathers and spiritual mothers. We all need to give birth to spiritual children and raise them. Apostle Paul reminds the Corinthian church that he is their spiritual father who gave birth to them.

> "Even if you had ten thousand guardians in Christ, you do not have many fathers, for in Christ Jesus I became your father through

the gospel" (1 Cor. 4:15).

There were many teachers who had spiritual influence on the Christians in the Corinthian church, but Apostle Paul tells them not to forget that he is their spiritual father who preached to them the Good News and raised them up according to the gospel. His desire was that one day he would see all the mature believers in the Corinthian church become spiritual fathers like him.

In *The Pilgrim's Progress*, after passing through the Wicket Gate with the help of Goodwill's guidance, Christian arrives at Interpreter's House. When Interpreter opens the door and welcomes Christian, what awaits him first is a portrait of a person appearing in dignity. His eyes are looking up to the sky as he is holding the book of books. On his lips are engraved the law of truth and on his head is the golden crown. John Bunyan was showing in the portrait someone like John Gifford, who interpreted the gospel to him and mentored him. This is why this house the pilgrim visits is called the Interpreter's House.

John Bunyan must have been thinking of the rectory where John Gifford used to welcome him and explain the gospel to him when describing the Interpreter's House. But the portrait at the entrance of this house does not only symbolize ordained priests or pastors but all mature spiritual fathers. Interpreter says that such are those who guide us to heaven. The following introduction of the house symbolizes the role of spiritual fathers who have the responsibility of spiritual direction. What exactly is the role of a spiritual father?

The Role of a Spiritual Father

First, a spiritual father teaches the power of the gospel.
After Interpreter shows Christian the shepherd's portrait, he takes him to the parlor. It looks as if it was not cleaned for a long time, and Interpreter calls a servant boy to clean it. As the servant starts sweeping the room, the room becomes full of dust, making it hard to breathe. Then he orders a servant girl beside him to fetch water and sprinkle it all over the room. When she sprinkles the water, the dust slowly dissipates, and the room soon finds calm and peace. When Christian asks what it means, Interpreter explains that the dust signifies man's sin, and the sweeping servant symbolizes the teaching of the law. The law evokes sin and therefore leads us to repentance, but it does not solve the problem of sin. On the other hand, the servant girl who sprinkles water symbolizes the gospel. Only the gospel can remove sin in man's heart and transform it

into a place worthy for the King to dwell in.

Mature spiritual fathers need to teach young souls the power of this gospel. The law or morality have failed to change mankind. Degrading Christianity as a religion of law, a moral religion, or even an ethical value system is no different from sweeping a room full of dust. The verse that John Bunyan quotes in this part is Romans 7:6.

> "But now, by dying to what once bound us, we have been released from the law so that we serve in the new way of the Spirit, and not in the old way of the written code."

Nevertheless, the Bible teaches us the reason that the law exists.

> "What shall we say, then? Is the law sinful? Certainly not! Nevertheless, I would not have known what sin was had it not been for the law. For I would not have known what coveting really was if the law had not said, 'You shall not covet'" (Rom. 7:7).

That's right. Through the law, we become conscious of our sins that we commit by breaking it, and therefore we become dead before God. But in order to break away from these sins, we need to sprinkle water, rather than sweep the dust. Water in this part indicates the gospel. The moment we accept Jesus Christ who is the Good News, we are forgiven of our sins and recover peace in our souls. Therefore, what we need to hold onto is not the law but the gospel that has been delivered to us by the power of the Holy Spirit. All spiritual fathers need to have the conviction that only this power of the gospel can change man.

Second, a spiritual father teaches the reward of patience.

Interpreter leads Christian to a small room where two children are each sitting on a chair. One looks discontent while the other seems at peace. The grumpy one is called Passion and the peaceful one is called Patience. Christian asks Interpreter, "What is the reason of the discontent of Passion?" Interpreter replies, "The governor of them would have him stay for his best things till the beginning of next year; but he will have all now. Patience is willing to wait." Interpreter then says that Passion symbolizes those who belong to the world, and Patience the people of God's Kingdom.

What does this mean? What true Christians need to learn throughout their lifetime is the lesson of patience. Those who become God's people are given so many blessed promises. Yet, the many promises are not to be enjoyed right away, but they are rather a portion that can be enjoyed through the journey of maturity, which takes time. It is an inheritance that we will enjoy in the eternal Kingdom and not on this earth. Hence, such inheritance is a reward only attainable through patience.

One important spiritual discipline that we need to learn after we become Christians is training ourselves to see the world that is unseen rather than the one seen. Heaven is the eventual reward given to those who know how to wait for the coming hope rather than the happiness that can be earned right away. In this part Interpreter introduces 2 Corinthians 4:18 to Christian.

> "So we fix our eyes not on what is seen, but on what is unseen, since what is seen is temporary, but what is unseen is eternal."

How does the author of Hebrews explain the essence of faith?

> "Now faith is confidence in what we hope for and assurance about what we do not see"(Heb. 11:1).

> "And without faith it is impossible to please God, because anyone who comes to him must believe that he exists and that he rewards those who earnestly seek him"(Heb. 11:6).

If we have such faith, we can be patient. And we will finally enjoy the full reward. The essence of heaven is receiving the reward of patience. What spiritual fathers need to teach spiritual children is also this reward of patience. Heaven is a place that can be enjoyed only through patience.

Third, a spiritual father teaches the ministry of grace.

Interpreter then takes Christian to a room where there is a fireplace. As the fire in the furnace is blazing up, someone pours water on it to quench the fire. However, the flame does not die out but keeps burning. It is because there is someone who continuously fuels the fire with oil on the other side of the wall. Christian asks, "What does this mean?" Interpreter says that the one who pours water to put out the fire is the Devil. And the one who is fueling the oil is Christ.

One of the important ministries of Christ is pouring the oil of grace on the hearts of Christians so that the ministry of grace can continue. This is why the word "Christ" means "the anointed one." He was able to endure the ministry of the Savior as the Messiah because He was anointed.

"How God anointed Jesus of Nazareth with the Holy Spirit and

> power, and how he went around doing good and healing all who were under the power of the devil, because God was with him" (Acts 10:38).

Having been resurrected, raised up to Heaven, and seated at the right hand of God, Jesus is now the one who anoints God's people to help them. In this part Bunyan quotes 2 Corinthians 12:9.

> "But he said to me, 'My grace is sufficient for you, for my power is made perfect in weakness.' Therefore I will boast all the more gladly about my weaknesses, so that Christ's power may rest on me."

Apostle Paul was God's precious servant, but he had a physical thorn and therefore was always in pain. He sincerely petitioned to God three times to remove the physical thorn, but the thorn did not disappear as he had expected. Nevertheless, he endured the pain and went around the world more than three times to preach the gospel, carrying out his mission of building churches everywhere he went. It was thanks to Christ's ministry of grace that was pouring oil onto Paul's heart. We need to believe in this ministry of grace. We need to believe in the ministry of the Holy Spirit, the spirit of Christ, who works to guard the grace started in us and to share this grace with others.

Without such ministry, the preaching of the gospel or going on missions is in vain. Our spiritual forefathers called this ministry of grace the "doctrine of perseverance of the saints" or the "doctrine of eternal security."

Let's remind ourselves of the message that Apostle Paul gave to his spiritual son Timothy in 2 Timothy 1 as a spiritual father.

> "For this reason I remind you to fan into flame the gift of God, which is in you through the laying on of my hands. For the Spirit God gave us does not make us timid, but gives us power, love and self-discipline" (2 Tim. 1:6-7).

In these days we need to pray that Christ's anointing and His ministry of grace would be present everywhere the gospel is preached and among all those who have new life. We need to hope that even more spiritual fathers and spiritual mothers will rise up. We must first willingly devote ourselves to preparing to live as a spiritual father and mother. May God bless all those who labor as spiritual fathers and mothers in Christ's name. I pray that we will all live as a spiritual father and mother.

Questions for the Pilgrimage of Faith

1. What are the three missions of a spiritual father?

1)

2)

3)

2. What do you need to have in order to become a good spiritual father or mother?

3. Is there anyone who has been a spiritual father or mother to you in your journey of faith? What did you learn from him or her?

4. How are the differences between legalism and the gospel, and between passion and patience, compared figuratively in *The Pilgrim's Progress*?

1 Thessalonians 2:6b-8 (NASB)

even though as apostles of Christ we might have asserted our authority. But we proved to be gentle among you, as a nursing mother tenderly cares for her own children. Having so fond an affection of you, we were well-pleased to impart to you not only the gospel of God but also our own lives, because you had become very dear to us.

1 Thessalonians 2:11-12 (NASB)

just as you know how we were exhorting and encouraging and imploring each one of you as a father would his own children, so that you would walk in a manner worthy of the God who calls you into His own kingdom and glory.

Pilgrim's Progress 10

Spiritual Direction

The Balance Between the Spiritual Mother and the Spiritual Father

One advertisement researcher asked the following question: "What is common between Madonna and Jodie Foster?" The answer is that they are both single parents. In the United States, 56 percent of families are single-parent families. In 2013 the average rate of single-parent families among OECD countries was 12.7 percent, and Korea averaged a little less at 11.5 percent.

Single-parent families refer to families that either do not have the mother or the father. A lot of problems that these families face are becoming serious social problems, but more than anything, we need to pay attention to the problems they have in rearing their children.

Healthy child-rearing is accomplished by experiencing the balance between the influence of a mother and that of a father, yet it is hard for single-parent families to do the same. This applies in the same way to our spiritual life. Healthy spiritual growth is also accomplished by the balanced influence of a spiritual mother and that of a spiritual father. If one only has a spiritual mother or a spiritual father, the spiritual parent has to play both roles.

Apostle Paul, during his second mission trip around AD 50-53 (which took approximately 3 weeks to 6 months), felt the need to write a series of mentoring letters to encourage the spiritual growth of the Thessalonian church. Hence, the letters that he wrote in Corinth are 1 and 2 Thessalonians. These letters have the characteristic of "spiritual guidance" or "spiritual direction."

Even during John Bunyan's time, spiritual direction had great significance. Richard Baxter, who was also a Puritan like John Bunyan, teaches in his book, *The Reformed Pastor*, that we should not be lazy with giving spiritual direction to those who are spiritually weak and immature. It was for this same reason that John Bunyan, in *The Pilgrim's Progress*, invites Christian to the Interpreter's house after he passes through the Wicket Gate. The portrait that he sees on the wall as soon as he enters the house is the portrait of a spiritual director, and the following rooms provide him with spiritual direction.

However, the characteristics of such direction are divided into two major kinds: those of encouragement and those of warning. If encouragement is the role of the spiritual mother, warning is the role of the spiritual father. If only warning without any encouragement is given to young souls, they will not be able to grow healthily with self-respect. On the other hand, if only encouragement is given and no appropriate warning is given, they will become self-indulgent and twisted. This is why the two kinds of spiritual mentorship are equally required.

Let's go back to the Interpreter's house and look at spiritual direction through the remaining rooms. Here we see two kinds of spiritual direction needed by those we share the gospel with.

Two Kinds of Spiritual Direction

First is the supply of hope through the love of the spiritual mother.

Rather than claiming his spiritual authority as an apostle of Christ, Apostle Paul confesses that he will approach the Christians in the Thessalonian church with a heart of a spiritual nursing mother.

> "…even though as apostles of Christ we might have asserted our authority. But we proved to be gentle among you, as a nursing mother tenderly cares for her own children" (1 Thess. 2:6b-7, NASB).

And he reminds them of the love that he showed them with the heart of a nursing mother:

> "Having so fond an affection for you, we were well-pleased to impart to you not only the gospel of God but also our own lives, because you had become very dear to us" (1 Thess. 2:8, NASB).

A love that gives not only the gospel, but also one's own life! Is this not the kind of love that we have seen in our mothers? Mothers do not stop at their sacrifice, but continue to go on to open doors for their children's future. This is why Apostle Paul wanted to see hope as well as the labor of love in the Thessalonian Church.

> "We remember before our God and Father your work produced by faith, your labor prompted by love, and your endurance inspired by hope in our Lord Jesus Christ"(1 Thess. 1:3).

That's right. He expected the labor of love to lead to the endurance of hope. We see that John Bunyan wanted to give Christian this endurance of hope in the Interpreter's house. After visiting the room with the furnace, Interpreter brings Christian to a solemn palace, a beautiful and splendid palace. The problem is that there are heavily-armed soldiers blocking the entrance. But then, a man with a sword and a helmet on his head courageously makes a way, and the gate opens with a choir resonating from above the palace walls.

"Come in, come in; Eternal glory thou shalt win."

As this brave man passes through the gate, golden garments are put on him. John Bunyan quotes Acts 14:22 in this part:

> "…strengthening the disciples and encouraging them to remain true to the faith. 'We must go through many hardships to enter the kingdom of God,' they said"(Acts 14:22).

125

This is supplying the endurance of hope through love. John Bunyan probably had 2 Timothy 4 in mind:

> "I have fought the good fight, I have finished the race, I have kept the faith. Now there is in store for me the crown of righteousness, which the Lord, the righteous Judge, will award to me on that day—and not only to me, but also to all who have longed for his appearing" (2 Tim. 4:7-8).

Do you feel the encouragement to keep going and look towards hope? How would Christian reply to this scene? He smiles and says, "I think verily I know the meaning of this. Now let me go hence."

Then the Interpreter tells him that he cannot leave yet for he has one more thing to show him. His spiritual direction has not yet finished. The rest of what Christian is going to see at the Interpreter's house is the message of warning.

Second is the warning lesson given through the spiritual father's discipline.

Apostle Paul did not want to remain only as a spiritual mother to Christians in the Thessalonian church. He wanted to willingly take the role of a spiritual father for their healthy spiritual growth.

> "…just as you know how we were exhorting and encouraging and imploring each of you as a father would his own children"(1 Thess. 2:11, NASB).

The most important roles of the spiritual father here are exhortation and caution because encouragement can be received from the spiritual mother. Why do we need exhortation and caution?

> "…so that you would walk in a manner worthy of the God who calls you into His own kingdom and glory"(1 Thess. 2:12, NASB).

The reason we need exhortation and caution is so that we can gloriously enter the Kingdom of God, our final destination. Sometimes exhortation and caution are hard and painful to take in, yet are so necessary for us. The disappearance of exhortation and caution in today's education is not desirable for the future of our children.

At the Interpreter's house we encounter two images that we need to watch out for. The first one is the "man in an iron cage." He is looking to the ground with his sorrowful head bowed in a very dark room. Time to time he releases sighs as if his heart would break. Christian asks him, "Who are you?"

He replies, "I am what I was not once. I was once, as I thought, fair for the Celestial City, and had even joy at the thoughts that I should get thither. I gave in to the temptation of the Devil and rushed after my own lusts. Now I am stuck in this cage of despair."

Then he cries out, "I have crucified Him to myself afresh. I have despised His person. I have despised His holiness; I have counted His blood an unholy thing; I have shown contempt to the Spirit of mercy. Now even if I read His Word, my faith is not restored, and even if I want to repent, I cannot repent."

Then the Interpreter says to Christian, "Remember this man's misery. Even Christians can end up here."

To this Christian replies, "I will be watchful and pray." At this moment, Interpreter tells Christian that there is one more thing that he needs to see.

The second scene that they see is a "man trembling in his bedroom." As Interpreter asks the man to explain why he is trembling so badly, his confession begins.

"I dreamed, and behold, the heavens grew exceeding black; also it thundered and lightened in most fearful manner, that it put me into an agony. So I looked up in my dream, and saw the clouds rack at an unusual rate; upon which I heard a great sound of a trumpet, and saw also a Man sitting upon a cloud, saying, 'Arise, ye dead, and come to judgment.' The wheat and the tares were separated, and heaven and hell split. My sins came into my mind, and my conscience accused me without mercy. I was not ready to stand before the judgment seat. I could not bear to see the face of the angry Judge."

Then Interpreter asks Christian, "Hast thou considered these things?"

Christian honestly replies, "Yes; and they put me in hope and fear."

Interpreter tells him seriously, "That's right. Hope and fear are gifts that come together. As you head to New Jerusalem, remember these things and meditate on them. I hope that you will be strengthened by the hope of the Kingdom. Yet, walk in fear and trembling that you would not be embarrassed on the day of judgment."

Just as the Interpreter urges Christian, what we need is the rebuke of our spiritual fathers.

> "A wise son heeds his father's instruction, but a mocker does not respond to rebukes" (Prov. 13:1).

If spiritual direction is restored once again in this generation, Christians of this generation will experience spiritual revival. Godly fear is a gift of God that propels sanctification. This generation is a generation that has lost godly fear and so we are living in spiritual prisons where there is neither repentance nor restoration. We need to recover holiness in order to have true spiritual freedom. What Christians of this generation need is not happiness, but holiness.

Francis A. Schaeffer, Christian philosopher of L'Abri and evangelist, cried out before his death during his last prophetic sermon, "The tragedy of our generation is that the people of God desire for happiness, but no longer desire holiness."

What we need in order to have hunger for holiness is godly fear. We need the assurance of salvation, but Christians also need to remember that judgment, which will hold them accountable for how they lived here, awaits. Do not forget the message that Apostle Paul gave to the Corinthian church, which struggled with the snares of secularization:

> "Therefore, since we have these promises, dear friends, let us purify ourselves from everything that contaminates body and spirit, perfecting holiness out of reverence for God" (2 Cor. 7:1).

We will live if we remember the spiritual father's rebukes. If we hold onto these lessons of caution, we will surely one day meet the day of glory. Our road of pilgrimage will be a road of victory. But if we forget this warning, we may be caged with shame. We may tremble as we wait for the day of judgment on our deathbeds.

What is your choice? Will you follow spiritual direction and obey? At the same time, will you also be someone else's spiritual director? The choice is on us. Yet, the choice that we make will determine our eternal destiny.

Questions for the Pilgrimage of Faith

1. What are the things that a spiritual mother should provide for her children?

2. What are the things that a spiritual father should provide for his children?

3. There are two images of warning that Christian looks into at Interpreter's House. What do the "man in an iron cage" and the "man trembling in the bedroom" mean?

4. What are the two things we need for true spiritual freedom?

If spiritual direction is restored once again in this generation,

Christians of this generation will experience spiritual revival.

Godly fear is a gift of God that propels sanctification.

Proverbs 5:22-23

The evil deeds of the wicked ensnare them; the cords of their sins hold them fast. For lack of discipline they will die, led astray by his own great folly.

Proverbs 6:9

How long will you lie there, you sluggard? When will you get up from your sleep?

Pilgrim's Progress 11

Sleeping Man

The Meaning of Spiritual Sleep

While we live in this world, the most important factor for our health is to sleep soundly, that is getting a good night's rest. Sleep is the foundation of our daily activities. As we sleep, our bodies are relieved of fatigue, detoxified from harmful substances, and recharged with energy. Our body goes through a physiological activity useful for secreting different hormones in our bodies. Therefore, the Bible states that "he grants sleep to those he loves" (Ps. 127:2).

Being unable to sleep well is a distressing pain that is difficult to overcome. The greatest torture is not being allowed to sleep. Although the Bible explains physical sleep as rest, in comparison it states that spiritual sleep can be very dangerous. It warns us, when the Lord returns to this earth, to "not let him find you sleeping"(Mark 13:36) and to "do this, understanding the present time: The hour has come for you to wake up from your slumber"(Rom. 13:11). In 1 Corinthians 11, as the Apostle Paul teaches the church in Corinth to live a consecrated life worthy in taking the Lord's Supper, he also warns those who are unprepared, saying "That is why many among you are weak and sick, and a number of you have fallen asleep"(verse 30).

Falling asleep spiritually is extremely dangerous as it is the road that leads to death. The danger of falling into spiritual sleep can exist even for those who have experienced the cross and have started their pilgrimage of faith. John Bunyan continues to explain this truth through the story of *The Pilgrim's Progress*.

Not long after Christian the pilgrim passes the cross, he spots three men sleeping on the road with their ankles chained up. John Bunyan quotes the following Bible verse to express the danger these men are in.

> "You will be like one sleeping on the high seas, lying on top of the rigging" (Prov. 23:34).

Although it may seem as though they are enjoying the moment, the reality is that they are in the state right before sinking, right before death. How did they end up in this state? We can find the reasons believers fall into spiritual sleep within the names of the three people who are chained up. What is the cause of "spiritual sleep" suggested by the names of these three people?

The Three Types of People Who Are Spiritually Asleep

The first type is "Simple."

John Bunyan calls the first person who is asleep, "Simple." In the English language, the word "simple" can have both positive and negative meanings. Here, it is being used in a negative manner. It depicts a person who is so simple that they have lost the ability to discern the matters of life. In Korean slang, this can be referred to as a "pickled radish life" (*dan-moo-ji* life). *Dan* means "simple" and *moo-ji* means "foolish". It is a simple but foolish way of living.

This person cannot see the dangers right in front of him. It is like a patient who cannot perceive any detectable symptoms. The reason cancer treatment is difficult in many cases is that patients do not have any subjective symptoms. By the time patients become aware of the symptoms, it is often already too late to start treatment.

As Simple is awakened by Christian, he replies, "What's the fuss? I see no danger."

Even today, are there any who are like Simple? Are there any of us who find it cumbersome when someone is trying to wake us up because they see danger signals in our life? Most likely, these are people who rarely reflect upon their own lives. The reason we need Quiet Time, or a time of devotion, is that it allows us to look back upon our lives regularly in the presence of God. What do you think caused Simple to sleep on the road in chains? We can find the answer in Proverbs 5.

> "The evil deeds of the wicked ensnare them; the cords of their sins hold them fast. For lack of discipline they will die, led astray by their own great folly" (Prov. 5:22-23).

Because he distanced himself from the discipline of the Word, his spirit eventually had fallen asleep and could not break free from the sin in which he was entangled. Isn't our spiritual state also facing such foolishness? Yet, aren't we telling ourselves, "I don't have any problem?" This is what we call the "dan-moo-ji life."

The second type is "Sloth."

In *The Pilgrim's Progress*, John Bunyan depicts the second sleeping man as "Sloth" or "Laziness." It is certain that John Bunyan must have been thinking of Proverbs 6 as he described Sloth.

> "How long will you lie there, you sluggard? When will you get up from your sleep? A little sleep, a little slumber, a little folding of the hands to rest" (Prov. 6:9-10).

In fact, if you read this portion in *The Pilgrim's Progress*, as Christian wakes up the second sleeping man, he responds in this manner: "I just need a little more sleep." He does not care about what is going on in the world and is satisfied as long as he can sleep just a little more. In today's Korean humor, this lifestyle is called the "sausage life" (*so-sae-ji* life). A deserted (*so*), renouncing the world (*sae*), and fed up (*ji*) kind of life. Why have our lives come to this state? It is because we have given up on our futures, on our tomorrow.

There are many Christians who have fallen into a spiritual sleep and have given up on their tomorrow. This is due to a lack of faith, or having little faith. These people no longer trust in God. They do not believe that God has prepared a better future for them. They find no reason to sweat and work hard for their future. Their only reason for living is to be able to sleep a little more or eat a little more right in this moment. What warning is given to those who live this kind of life?

> "And poverty will come on you like a thief and scarcity like an armed man" (Prov. 6:11).

Sloth, namely laziness, will eventually steal the comfort and freedom of those who want to sleep and eat just a little more. This is why the author of Proverbs uses the ant, the God-sent teacher, to warn those who are asleep.

> "Go to the ant, you sluggard; consider its ways and be wise!" (Proverbs 6:6).

What is the nature of wisdom that belongs to the ant?

> "Yet it stores its provisions in summer and gathers its food at harvest" (Prov. 6:8).

The ant is a future-oriented being. He diligently looks towards tomorrow and prepares for it. In that sense, a life that does not prepare for tomorrow is worth less than the life of an ant. Christians have a greater responsibility than just preparing for what they will eat. Christians need to live their lives in preparation to stand before God. However, those who are spiritually asleep and live a lazy lifestyle do not even consider being prepared. The Bible continues to tell such people, "Wake up!" We need to wake up and get ready. Christians need to prepare their lives to be unashamed when they stand before the judgment of God.

The third type is "Presumption."

John Bunyan calls the third sleeping man "Presumption." When Christian wakes him up, he responds, "Every tub must stand upon his own bottom."

In a modern English version, it is written in this manner: "I can make it myself without any help from you."

He is telling Christian not to interfere with his life, for he can take care of it himself. Does this not portray a prideful life? In today's humor, this lifestyle can be expressed as the "pickled cucumber life"(o*h-ee-ji* life). *Oh* stands for proud, *ee* stands for selfish and *ji* is short for someone who is self-centered. In other words, an "oh-ee-ji life" is one that is self-centered, proud, and cares only about oneself.

Today, if there is one worldview that strongly dominates our thoughts, it would be "secular humanism." There was a British poet who inspired this secular humanistic worldview. His name was William Ernest Henley. A line from one of his poems inspired many people to become secular humanists. Surprisingly, many people in the church also admire this poem.

"I am the master of my fate. I am the captain of my soul."

Take a close look at what this poem implies. If we are true Christians, we can neither agree with this poem nor should we do so. Why is this? Because we have already tried to be the master of our lives and the captain of our souls and have realized that living this way does not give us peace or any answers. It is because one day we came before the cross of Jesus Christ, to the one who died for our sins, and confessed, "You, You only are the master of my fate. You only are the captain of my soul." Apostle Paul makes a confession that is completely the opposite of Henley's poem.

> "I have been crucified with Christ and I no longer live, but Christ lives in me. The life I live in the body, I live by faith in the Son of God, who loved me and gave himself for me"(Gal. 2:20).

What is the core of this verse? It is that Christ alone is the master of my fate and the captain of my soul. But as we walk our journey of faith in Christ, we often forget that Christ is our master, and we find ourselves living according to our heart's desires. It is at this moment that we know we have fallen into a spiritual sleep. We have committed treason, as our pride and presumption have taken Jesus off the master's seat, and we have become the master of our lives once again. Who is responsible for this? It is a scheme of the evil one.

In *The Pilgrim's Progress*, Christian the pilgrim wakes sleeping Presumption and says, "Be self-controlled and alert. Your enemy the devil prowls around like a roaring lion looking for someone to devour"(1 Pet. 5:8). Wake up, and commit your life to the One who is your Master. Walk with Christ as he leads and guides you on this journey.

I hope that we will all be able to take part in the evangelization work to awaken all those who have fallen asleep and encourage them to join our pilgrimage. I pray that the Pilgrim's Progress Pilgrimage Park will be a spiritual road that awakens many who have spiritually fallen asleep.

that is completely the opposite of Henley's poem.

> "I have been crucified with Christ and I no longer live, but Christ lives in me. The life I live in the body, I live by faith in the Son of God, who loved me and gave himself for me" (Gal. 2:20).

What is the core of this verse? It is that Christ alone is the master of my fate and the captain of my soul. But as we walk our journey of faith in Christ, we often forget that Christ is our master, and we find ourselves living according to our heart's desires. It is at this moment that we know we have fallen into a spiritual sleep. We have committed treason, as our pride and presumption have taken Jesus off the master's seat, and we have become the master of our lives once again. Who is responsible for this? It is a scheme of the evil one.

In *The Pilgrim's Progress*, Christian the pilgrim wakes sleeping Presumption and says, "Be self-controlled and alert. Your enemy the devil prowls around like a roaring lion looking for someone to devour" (1 Pet. 5:8). Wake up, and commit your life to the One who is your Master. Walk with Christ as he leads and guides you on this journey.

I hope that we will all be able to take part in the evangelization work to awaken all those who have fallen asleep and encourage them to join our pilgrimage. I pray that the Pilgrim's Progress Pilgrimage Park will be a spiritual road that awakens many who have spiritually fallen asleep.

Questions for the Pilgrimage of Faith

1. Write about the three types of people who have fallen asleep spiritually.

1)

2)

3)

2. Reflect upon your life and see if there was a time in which you were in the crisis of falling into a spiritual sleep.

3. What do we need to do in order to not become spiritually ignorant?

4. What do we need to do to live a humble and alert life that is future-oriented like the ant's?

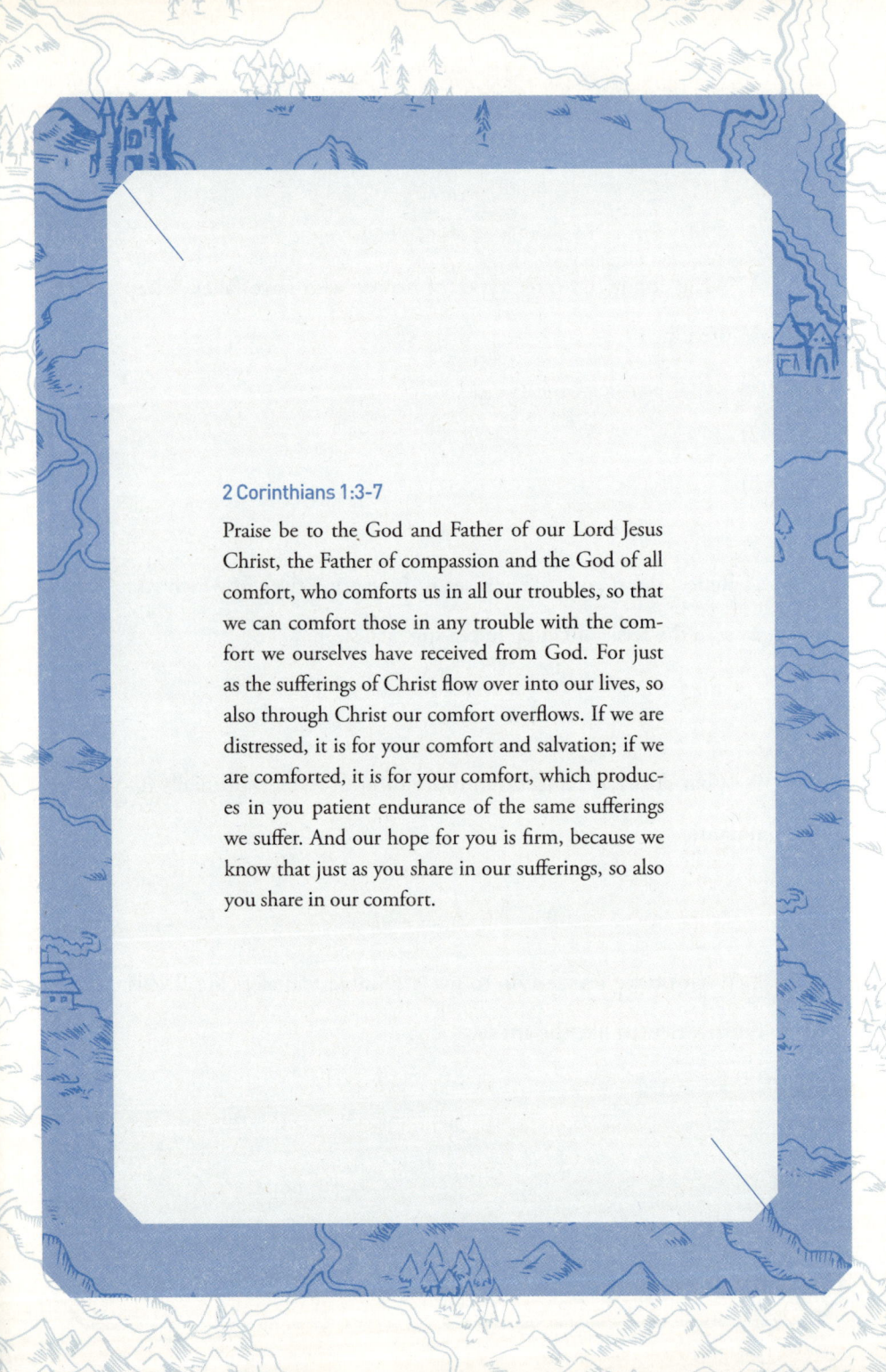

2 Corinthians 1:3-7

Praise be to the God and Father of our Lord Jesus Christ, the Father of compassion and the God of all comfort, who comforts us in all our troubles, so that we can comfort those in any trouble with the comfort we ourselves have received from God. For just as the sufferings of Christ flow over into our lives, so also through Christ our comfort overflows. If we are distressed, it is for your comfort and salvation; if we are comforted, it is for your comfort, which produces in you patient endurance of the same sufferings we suffer. And our hope for you is firm, because we know that just as you share in our sufferings, so also you share in our comfort.

Pilgrim's Progress 12

Hill Difficulty

Theology of the Cross vs. Theology of Prosperity

The sole foundation for the faith of evangelical Christians is always the Bible. However, different theological views formulate depending on how Scripture is interpreted to provide Christians with practical, real-life perspectives on life. Of these, there are two contrasting theologies that have especially had an influence on the formation of the Christian faith. The first is the "theology of the cross" and the other is the "theology of prosperity." These two theological stances have strictly conflicting views about suffering and hardships in life.

A well-known motto for the "theology of the cross" is "No cross, no crown." In order to one day receive the crown that the Lord will bestow upon us, we need to willingly take up our cross and endure suffering. This confession was the core of the Puritan theology and the theological basis for *The Pilgrim's Progress*.

However, a recent trend of theology that contradicts this theological perspective has risen. We call it the "prosperity theology." It was primarily started by groups of people who "excessively" emphasize spiritual gifts. The motto that represents the prosperity theology is "Nothing is impossible." They state that, if we truly believe in an almighty God, we should not accept suffering. They claim that it is never God's will for those who believe in Jesus to be sick and poor and fail in life. A normal life for those who believe in Jesus should include physical health, financial wealth, and success in our society. That is why the prosperity theology is also called "health and wealth gospel," "prosperity gospel," or "gospel of success."

Those who have been influenced by this type of theology naturally believe that people who are poor or fighting a disease are under the rule of the devil. They also show a tendency in trying to find the core of their faith in earthly, materialistic blessings and success. Generally, those whose faith is very unstable despite the fact that they are Christians are likely influenced by the prosperity theology. These two contrasting theologies produce two very different types of pilgrims that live on this earth.

As we read *The Pilgrim's Progress*, we meet many people on the journey from the cross to House Beautiful. We can also see two contrasting tendencies in these pilgrims. Conspicuously, these two groups of people are divided at the Hill Difficulty. Who are these two types of pilgrims?

Pilgrims We Meet at the Foot of Hill Difficulty

First, there are pilgrims who choose the easier-looking "curved path."

For those representing the pilgrims who have chosen this path, John Bunyan calls them "Formalist" and "Hypocrisy." As these pilgrims come to the foot of the Hill Difficulty, they choose the easy-looking paths on both the right and left sides, rather than the straight but steep path that leads up the hill. They believe that these two paths will eventually lead to Mount Zion. However, the name of the path that they choose is in fact "Danger and Destruction." Their pilgrimage eventually ends in destruction. While he is walking on the comfortable path, Hypocrisy stumbles on a jagged rock, falls and gives up on his journey. This passage of the story shows us that the road that seems comfortable to our eyes never leads to the right path.

In fact, Formalist and Hypocrisy did not enter through the Wicket Gate but climbed over the wall. When Christian asks them if they have not read that "the man who does not enter by the gate is a thief and a robber"(John 10:1), they answer that it is a waste of energy to enter through the narrow gate when it is much easier to climb over the wall. The most important thought that consumes their minds is to live an easy, convenient life.

These two pilgrims, Formalist and Hypocrisy, argue that everyone from their hometown live likewise. In the end, they just need to get to Mount Zion. They believe that their purpose justifies all means. This means that in order to achieve their goal, the methods they use do not matter as long as it is the quickest and the easiest way. The road they choose is the curved path that looks easy to the eyes.

There are also other pilgrims we meet on this curved path. John Bunyan calls them "Timorous" and "Mistrust." Just as Christian climbs over Hill Difficulty, he meets a group of pilgrims returning from the way they came. These pilgrims were Timorous and Mistrust. Timorous questions how they could ever finish their journey when they continue facing more and more dangers. He says that, hence, he would rather go back to the starting point. Meanwhile, Mistrust warns Christian that he will see a lion at a corner of the road if he continues down this road. His point is that they would end up as the lion's prey if they were to go on. The fear of difficulties that they might face in the future causes the pilgrims to turn and take the wrong path. John Bunyan ingeniously incorporates the lion based on Scripture.

> "A sluggard says, 'There is a lion in the road, a fierce lion roaming the streets!'" (Prov. 26:13).

These pilgrims were lazy and did not have courage to face any suffering. Seeking comfort is not bad in itself. However, if our selfish desire for comfort leads us to give up seeking spirituality, there is no greater tragedy as it leads us to unbelief rather than belief. There certainly are pilgrims today who are like Timorous and Mistrust. They enjoy the comfortable life and as a result of their laziness, they are prone to taking the easy-looking, curved road.

Second, there are pilgrims who choose the rugged but "straight path."

Christian, the main character of *The Pilgrim's Progress*, is an example. Before Christian reaches the foot of the Hill Difficulty, he has to walk the road from the narrow gate that leads to the steep and high path. Even though it is a difficult path, Christian thinks that he has to take it. He chooses the difficult path in silence. But just as he begins to walk this difficult path, he discovers a spring flowing with clear water at the bottom of the hill. Christian drinks from this spring until he is no longer thirsty. It is at this part that John Bunyan introduces Isaiah 49:10.

> "They will neither hunger nor thirst, nor will the desert heat or the sun beat upon them. He who has compassion on them will guide them and lead them beside springs of water."

Unquestionably, there is suffering on the pilgrims' journey, yet at the same time, there will also be sufficient encouragement that protects them.

Apostle Paul attests to this in 2 Corinthians chapter 1. In this short passage, the words "suffering" and "troubles" appear 6 times but the word "comfort" appears a total of 10 times. We cannot avoid troubles on our pilgrimage, but God's encouragement that overpowers our troubles is with us. That is why all pilgrims can continue on this road in faith. In the passage, Apostle Paul first of all praises God as the "God of all comfort."

> "Praise be to the God and Father of our Lord Jesus Christ, the Father of compassion and the God of all comfort" (2 Cor. 1:3).

He then writes that God is a God who comforts those who are suffering, and as a result, He expects those who experience His comfort to also live life as a comforter.

> "…who comforts us in all our troubles, so that we can comfort those in any trouble with the comfort we ourselves have received from God" (2 Cor. 1:4).

And finally in verse 5, we see the climax of Paul's confession.

> "For just as the sufferings of Christ flow over into our lives, so also our comfort abounds through Christ."

Returning to *The Pilgrim's Progress*, we meet the pilgrim who drinks from the spring of encouragement. He climbs the hill while singing praises, just as Apostle Paul did.

> "The hill, though high, I covet to ascend;
> The difficulty will not me offend,
> For I perceive the way to life lies here.
> Come, pluck up, heart, let's neither faint nor fear.
> Better, though difficult, the right way to go,
> Than wrong, though easy, where the end is woe."

Sure enough, Hill Difficulty is not an easy path. But Christian, who begins his journey with praise and prayer, climbs up the hill first running, then walking, and then clambering. When he is midway through, a pleasant arbor awaits him. It is at this place where he experiences the grace of God who prepares encouragement and rest for the journey. At the pleasant arbor, Christian takes out and reads the scroll that he kept in his bosom. He takes rest as he receives strength from the Word.

Nevertheless, John Bunyan warns that pilgrims should not put down their guard even while they experience encouragement and rest. Christian begins to doze off as he enjoys his rest. He eventually loses his scroll after falling asleep, proving that he is not an exception as he also loses the Word and falls into a spiritual sleep in a moment of carelessness. Because of this mistake, Christian has to climb back up the rough hill in order to find his scroll. Here, John Bunyan presents to the readers the following passage from the Bible.

> "Consider how far you have fallen! Repent and do the things you did at first. If you do not repent, I will come to you and remove your lampstand from its place"(Rev. 2:5).

The pilgrim, in tears, experiences restoring grace. Has there ever been a time when you lost the Word because you dozed off? The important truth is that you can climb up the hill again at any time. This road in Hill Difficulty will eventually lead us to the glory of Zion and to the King's throne in New Jerusalem.

Once I attended a KOSTA conference in Shanghai where I met a young pastor from America who ministered to African-Americans. He told me a saying many African-Americans like.

"The way to the throne room is through the thorn room."

It is true. No one can reach the throne of Zion without passing through Hill Difficulty. Remember the teaching that Apostle Paul gave to his fellow workers after experiencing hardships on his mission trip:

> "…strengthening the disciples and encouraging them to remain true to the faith. 'We must go through many hardships to enter the kingdom of God'" (Acts 14:22).

Ultimately, the message of this passage is: "No cross, no crown." This is the essence of the theology of the cross, the faith of the cross. Those who overcome the world and finish their race of faith will hold onto the ultimate hope through suffering and encouragement. It will be just as what Apostle Paul testified to in the passage.

> "And our hope for you is firm, because we know that just as you share in our sufferings, so also you share in our comfort" (2 Cor. 1:7).

What will you choose then? Will you choose the curved, easy-looking path? Or will you take the straight path, even if it is rugged? It is in climbing up the steep and straight path that God's true encouragement will be present. When we experience this encouragement, we will have the courage to fight the temptation of taking the comfortable path and walk the rough yet straight path.

Questions for the Pilgrimage of Faith

1. Who are the two contrasting types of pilgrims that we meet on the road to Hill Difficulty?

1)

2)

2. What are the two theologies that represent these two types of pilgrims?

1)

2)

3. Do you have a wavering faith that prosperity theology seeks after? What blessings are you asking God for?

4. In order to choose the straight but rugged path, without being blinded by the comfortable-looking path, what must we do?

1 Timothy 3:15

...if I am delayed, you will know how people ought to conduct themselves in God's household, which is the church of the living God, the pillar and foundation of the truth.

Pilgrim's Progress 13

House Beautiful

When world-renowned author Philip Yancey visited the Korean church, Global Mission Church held a seminar entitled "6 Hours with the Leaders of the Korean Church" at Pilgrim House. Of his many best selling books, one is entitled, *Church, My Love and My Worry*(IVP, 2010) in the Korean translation. There are probably many who can identify with this title. It is because this title embodies many feelings people have towards the church. The original title of this book is *Church: Why Bother?* In the preface of his book, Philip Yancey shares his heart with the readers of the Korean Church.

"Many might question the need for a book like this to the Korean church, which boasts of its global scale and dynamics. However, I believe there are just as many young people in Korea as those in Europe or in America who doubt and have fallen into skepticism about the church. Is there any reason that one should belong to an organization called a church? Can't we live a spiritual life even without religion? Isn't it enough that we have met God through Christianity? Why do we need to form relationships with other Christians whom we do not get along with?"

In this book, Philip Yancey confesses that he also once left the church after much disappointment. In spite of this, he has returned to the church and testifies that the church has become the love of his life and a fundamental portion of his life. In this book, he writes that if there exists the most beautiful analogy about the church, it would be "home" or "family."

He quotes the words of the famous poet Robert Frost who stated, "Home is the place where, when you have to go there, they have to take you in."

John Bunyan shared the same perspective. He sets "House Beautiful" as the place where the main character Christian gains rest and renewed strength during his trouble-filled journey. Even on this difficult journey, there is an unexpected stately palace that awaits him.

Even so, do you think John Bunyan was never hurt or disappointed by the church? Most likely he must have experienced such moments. Then what do you think is the reason he calls Christian's resting place, which symbolizes the church, "House Beautiful" despite his hurts and disappointments from the church? We will look at two reasons why the church can be a beautiful house.

Reasons that the Church can be a Beautiful House

First, the church is the pillar and foundation of the beautiful truth.

In 1 Timothy 3:15, Apostle Paul testifies that the church is the pillar and foundation of the truth.

> "If I am delayed, you will know how people ought to conduct themselves in God's household, which is the church of the living God, the pillar and foundation of the truth."

Here, Apostle Paul not only calls the church the house of the living God, but declares that it is the pillar and foundation of truth. Just as the pillar holds up the roof and the foundation holds up the whole building, the church holds up the glorious truth of the gospel.

Furthermore, Apostle Paul confesses, "How beautiful are the feet of those who bring good news"(Rom. 10:15). If the act of bringing the good news is beautiful, then the gospel in itself is an even more beautiful truth. In *The Pilgrim's Progress*, John Bunyan declares that the church, the place that protects and teaches the Gospel, is a beautiful house. Apostle Paul clarifies that this truth is not an ideological or philosophical truth, but Jesus Christ Himself.

> "Beyond all question, the mystery of godliness is great: He appeared in the flesh, was vindicated by the Spirit, was seen by angels, was preached among the nations, was believed on in the world, was taken up in glory"(1 Tim. 3:16).

The church is the house whose head is our beautiful Lord. Therefore, no one can truly become a part of this house or family without confessing that Jesus Christ is Lord. In *The Pilgrim's Progress*, as Christian asks if he can lodge at House Beautiful, the members of the household begin to ask Christian different questions to see if he is qualified to stay at the house. The heart of this test is to see whether Christian has faith in Christ, the master of the house.

During John Bunyan's time, if anyone wanted to become a part of the Puritan church family, they had to go through a process of answering several questions posed by existing members to prove that they are a person of faith. Especially in the Baptist church to which John Bunyan belonged, a qualification for church membership was a "confession of regeneration."

At first, as Christian waits to enter House Beautiful, he is afraid and wants to turn back. It is because there are two lions prowling around in the front of the house. At this moment, the gatekeeper of the lodge speaks to Christian.

"Fear not the lions, for they are chained, and are placed there for the trial of faith where it is, and for the finding out of those that have none: keep in the midst of the path, and no hurt shall come unto thee."

In the distant future, even when we enter heaven, the eternal house of God, there will be many who worry if they can really make it. Our enemy the devil will prowl around them like a roaring lion, telling them that they are not qualified to enter the house. However, if we believe that Jesus is Christ and if we have the assurance that Jesus is our Lord and Savior, we can boldly enter into heaven without anything to fear.

Why is this so? It is because Jesus Christ is our forgiveness, our salvation, and our eternal life. It is because He is the one who declared, "I am the way and the truth and the life" (John 14:6).

Second, the church is a beautiful community of fellowship.
In *The Pilgrim's Progress*, the names of those whom Christian meets at House Beautiful are "Prudence," "Discretion," "Piety," and "Charity." John Bunyan calls them "beautiful maidens," or in other words, beautiful people.

During his stay at the house, Christian has wonderful fellowship with them. For a long time, they talk about their experiences from their pilgrimage. This is what a testimony looks like. An important way of fellowship for Christians is sharing personal testimonies of faith with one another. Believers of the Early Church started fellowship by sharing their testimonies. Without a testimony, no believer was accepted into the church body or allowed to partake in communion. This tradition was renewed and solidified during the time of the Puritan church.

After a time of sharing testimonies, a meal is prepared and people sit around the table for fellowship dinner. They share delicious food and stories. In the Bible, this type of community fellowship is always praised as something beautiful.

> "How good and pleasant it is when God's people live together in unity!" (Ps. 133:1).

John Bunyan testifies that the core of their conversation is about the Lord of Hill Difficulty, the Lord of House Beautiful. Literally, this fellowship is a fellowship that exalts the beautiful Lord. It is through the spiritual rest and the putting on of spiritual armor that follow this fellowship that pilgrims can courageously continue their journey. This is what the church is all about.

However, some may question, "In reality, we don't always see this type of beautiful fellowship within the church, do we?" This is because they are reminded of relationships within the church that have hurt and disappointed them rather than encouraged them. Nevertheless, the church of Christ really is a beautiful house.

The answer can be found in Philip Yancey's book *Church, Why Bother?* In his book, Philip Yancey suggests that we imagine a family sitting around a table for fellowship. Among those sitting around the table, there are clever people, some who are stupid, some who are ugly, and some who are good-looking. Some have had great success while some have experienced failures. Some are healthy and some are physically challenged. And of those sitting around the table, there are people who have hurt us or caused us trouble. But still, are they not all part of the family? Yancey states that a healthy family is a family that does not bring down stronger members and at the same time builds up weaker members. Let's read a passage from Philip Yancey's book.

> "Family is the one human institution we have no choice over. We get in simply by being born, and as a result we are involuntarily thrown together with a menagerie of strange and unlike people. Church calls for another step: to voluntarily choose to band together with a strange menagerie because of a common bond in Jesus Christ. I have found that such a community more resembles a family than any other human institution. Henri Nouwen once defined a community as 'a place where the person you least want to live with always lives.'"

There will be those who question why we must get along and continue to work together with people we do not enjoy being with. It is through this community where weak people gather to learn forgiveness, learn love, and become a community that proclaims the glory of the God who saved us. This in fact is the true beauty of fellowship.

Performance by an Amateur Orchestra

Philip Yancey tells a touching anecdote about a high school in Evergreen, a small mountain town in Colorado, USA, where he was living. The school had the only orchestra in town. One autumn day, this orchestra had a chance to perform Beethoven's Ninth Symphony. Undoubtedly, this intricate piece was too difficult for this amateur orchestra. It could have appeared as a foolish performance. But can we say that this performance was meaningless? Philip Yancey reminds us that this orchestra, although comprised of unskilled musicians, was the only way some of the townspeople would have ever heard Beethoven's music.

Why did Philip Yancey use this illustration? Although the Lord knows that we are unprepared as a community to perform the symphony of the gospel entrusted to us, he believes that the church is the only vessel. Even in all its weakness, the church is the only community which the Lord has empowered to perform this symphony of the gospel. Our instruments may be broken or may not make the right sounds, but he still calls us to play the sounds of the gospel.

"I know your weaknesses better than anyone else. I pray that you become better instruments. Never forget. You are the only community that can make the sound of the gospel. Do not forget that you are the only ones that can together produce the sound of hope and the sound of salvation to this world. This is the church, the beautiful house of God."

Although we are unqualified and lacking in many ways, there are neighbors who need to hear the gospel through us today. Are you ready to share the gospel of the Lord everyday with those who need to hear it? For some, it may be the only opportunity they have to hear the good news. If we miss this opportunity, they may never be able to experience House Beautiful. For this reason, although we may be unskilled, I hope that we all become a part of the church, the only community that spreads the gospel, so that we may introduce House Beautiful.

Questions for the Pilgrimage of Faith

1. What are two reasons in which the church can be "House Beautiful"?

1)

2)

2. Discuss the healthy perspective we should have of the church, a community filled with weaknesses.

3. Have you truly confessed your faith in Jesus Christ? Have a time where you confess that you are born again.

4. It is said the church is no different from a family. Is there a member that annoys you? Or a member that hurts you or gives you a hard time? Come before God and pray for them.

Romans 5:1-2

Therefore, since we have been justified through faith, we have peace with God through our Lord Jesus Christ, through whom we have gained access by faith into this grace in which we now stand. And we boast in the hope of the glory of God.

Pilgrim's Progress 14

Blessing of Peace

Fear and Anxiety, Two Factors that Threaten Peace

A survey was conducted in the U.S. asking middle-aged adults what they needed the most as they enter old age. The number one answer by far was "peace of mind." I think the same results would be found in Korea as well. The most mentioned word in daily greetings all over the world is "peace." The Hebrews say *shalom*, the Arabs who fight the Hebrews say *salaam*, the ancient Greeks said *khairete*, the Chinese say *ping an*, and we say *annyeong hashimnikka? Pyongan hashimnikka?* (Are you well? Are you at peace?) as we greet each other. Such greetings of peace are, paradoxically, evidence that humanity has lost its most valuable internal peace.

Paul Tillich, an outstanding philosopher and theologian of our time, said that the two factors that fundamentally threaten human peace are fear and anxiety. However, he points out that anxiety is more difficult to deal with than fear because we can identify the object of our fear but cannot easily grasp the object of our anxiety. He said that anxiety has its origin in death. Knowing that we will eventually have to return to nothing, this sense of futility causes anxiety. However, from a biblical interpretation, human anxiety comes from the anxiety of confronting God who will hold us accountable after we die for the life we have lived. The reason that we are uneasy about facing God is that we are not ready. Do you, by any chance, think that you are ready to meet God the Creator and Judge?

The Bible points out that being ready to meet God is to be at peace with Him. The Bible teaches us that all people are born and start their lives without peace with God. This is because sin has separated us from God. Every anxiety we feel in life surely has sin lurking underneath. As long as the issue of sin is unresolved, no one can fully enjoy peace with oneself, with one's neighbors, nor with God.

The Boy Who Killed the Duck

I started going to church in my early twenties, and I can recall a story that my pastor often told. This story about a boy helped me believe in Jesus for the first time.

As summer vacation began, a boy and his younger sister went to stay with their grandmother who lived in the countryside. To pass this time of boredom, the boy made a slingshot. He fixed a rubber band on a tree branch and wanted to sling stones to catch birds. He got excited and pulled on the slingshot every time a bird was seen. But the clever birds knew beforehand and would fly away, making it impossible for the boy to catch them. The boy headed home, disappointed, and when he neared the front yard he saw the waddling duck that his grandmother was lovingly raising. He pulled out the slingshot from his pocket, placed a stone on it, and pulled. The flying stone hit the duck squarely on its head, and the duck fell on the spot.

The boy walked up to the duck and saw that it had died. It felt good that he hit it, but he was in anguish as he felt that he sinned against his grandmother by killing the duck. Scared, he told his younger sister what had happened and made her promise that she would keep it a secret. Then he buried the duck in a corner of the yard and acted as if nothing had happened.

Dinnertime came. The boy was eating but had no appetite because of his troubled conscience. He avoided eye contact with his grandmother and tried not to speak with her. After dinner was finally over, his younger sister told him to do the dishes.

When he told her that it was her job to do the dishes, his sister threatened him that she would tell their grandmother what he did. While doing the dishes, he felt pathetic thinking that he might be spending the whole summer as his sister's slave.

After much thought, he went over to his grandmother's room and knocked on the door. He told her the whole story. But to his surprise she said, "Don't worry. As I was cleaning the second floor earlier today, I saw you kill the duck and bury it. I have already forgiven you, so be at peace and go to sleep." His grandmother then hugged him and prayed a prayer of blessing over him.

How happy do you think the boy was? He must have felt light-hearted, peaceful, and free. He had a good night's sleep, a delicious breakfast the next morning, and was not afraid when his sister told him to do the dishes and tried to threaten him. He was already at peace and had freedom from the night before.

In this passage in Romans 5, Apostle Paul declares that the same thing happens to Christians. Just as the boy who killed the duck tried to avoid his grandmother, we have run away from God in our sin. Just as the boy was a slave to his sister for a short while, we lived as slaves to the devil, condemning ourselves. We lived without peace in our hearts. This is the reality of a sinner. No matter what we do, there is no joy or peace.

Romans 5:1 says that we received forgiveness through Jesus, and now we have peace with God. This is the most noble blessing that man can ever experience.

> "Therefore, since we have been justified through faith, we have peace with God through our Lord Jesus Christ."

Romans 5:8 tells us that while we were still sinners, Jesus bore the punishment for our sins, and through His sacrifice we have been reconciled to God. The blessing that we have experienced is not only that we are forgiven but also that we are justified. This justification signifies that He sees us as though we have never sinned. We call this grace. Grace is God's love given to those who are unworthy to receive it. We have peace with God because of Jesus's love for us. This is the essence of the gospel.

Rest in the Chamber of Peace

In *The Pilgrim's Progress*, after walking on many paths of hardship, Christian finally climbs over Hill Difficulty and arrives at House Beautiful. The very first thing that he experiences upon entering the house is peace. He experiences rest that he has never experienced before and enjoys true rest in the chamber named "Peace" where a big window faces the sunrise. On the door of this chamber is written, "Peace." He takes rest until the break of day and awakes, singing:

> "Where am I now? Is this the love and care
> Of Jesus, for the men that pilgrims are,
> Thus to provide that I should be forgiven,
> And dwell already the next door to heaven?"

This song portrays the peace of forgiveness of sin and rest for the soul experienced by those who encounter Jesus in life's sufferings.

This peace can be experienced through Jesus alone. Do we not also need this kind of peace?

Believing in Jesus does not stop at the forgiveness of sin and peace of mind. Christian experiences various kinds of grace at House Beautiful. We who are now at peace with God must enter into a life that enjoys His grace more concretely. Romans 5:2 gives us this promise:

> "…through whom we have gained access by faith into this grace in which we now stand. And we boast in the hope of the glory of God."

We saw earlier that grace is God's love for those who are not worthy of His love. What would God hold back from us when He did not spare His one and only Son so that we may be reconciled to Him and live by grace?

> "He who did not spare his own Son, but gave him up for us all—how will he not also, along with him, graciously give us all things?" (Rom. 8:32).

The boy's grandmother did not condemn her grandson but

forgave him for killing the duck. Moreover, she hugged him and blessed him. The peace with his grandmother was the beginning of all blessings for him.

The Father Who Embraced the Prodigal Son

Let's think about the parable of the prodigal son which we are all familiar with. Breaking his father's heart by demanding his portion of the inheritance, the second son went away to a far country and squandered all his possessions. In those days, according to Middle Eastern customs, asking for an inheritance while the father was still alive was equivalent to telling him to die. The prodigal son needed forgiveness of sin in order to restore his relationship with his father. But the father, without any commotion or reproach, held his son in his arms and kissed him. It was a sign of unconditional forgiveness. It did not stop there, as the father put a ring on the son's finger, clothed him with new clothes, and put new shoes on his feet. He restored the son's status and blessed the beginning of his new life. He also gave a feast declaring, "My son was once dead and is alive again, was lost and has been found."

The Return of the Prodigal Son, a masterpiece by the great arts master Rembrandt Harmenszoon van Rijn, probably best depicts the Father's love for the prodigal son. Rembrandt was in his old age when he worked on this painting. He had lost his son and his older daughter. Soon after, his younger daughter also passed away. Then his wife died. Although he remarried, his second wife also passed away. In addition to losing wealth and fame, he was in great debt. Later, even his only remaining son Titus died. He was left all alone in despair. It was then that he realized he was the prodigal son and painted this painting.

The returning son whose head is shaved shows his impoverished reality, which illustrates starting over as a baby and returning to the Creator's arms. The single loose garment covering his gaunt body, his shoeless left foot, and a worn down sandal on the other foot show the time he spent wandering. In spite of all this, the father lovingly caresses the son who feebly leans into the father's embrace. His left arm shows his promise that he will never let go again. The right arm that is patting the son gently on his back is the tender arm of mercy. His cape is spread out widely towards his son. The rays from his face flow through his two hands and cover his son's whole body. With his dim and aged eyes, he looks into his son's far future and blesses him.

The son finally returned to his soul's home after a long time, returning to God the Father's arms. Borrowing from John Bunyan's words, he returned to the beautiful spiritual house where true peace awaited him. Rembrandt finally met God who wiped away his tears, and he was able to walk his final path of life in peace and rest.

Blessed is the feast prepared for those who seek such peace and rest. Listen to the invitation of Jesus, the Son of God.

> "Come to me, all you who are weary and burdened, and I will give you rest"(Matt. 11:28).

Also, Jesus promised this before going to the cross, bearing our sins upon Himself:

> "I am the way and the truth and the life. No one comes to the Father except through me"(John 14:6).

Questions for the Pilgrimage of Faith

1. What is the essence of peace experienced in the chamber of peace at House Beautiful?

2. What do we need to do in order to enjoy this peace?

3. Are you still living as a slave to sin? How can you break away from sin?

4. Meditate on Rembrandt's painting *The Return of the Prodigal Son*. Imagine God the Father embracing us as we return to Him from sin. Can you feel the grace of this blessing?

Hebrews 11:1-3

Now faith is confidence in what we hope for and assurance about what we do not see. This is what the ancients were commended for. By faith we understand that the universe was formed at God's command, so that what is seen was not made out of what was visible.

Pilgrim's Progress 15

Blessing of Faith

Chapter of Faith

On occasions when we share the Gospel, we hear quite a few people say, "I want to believe, but I just can't." The truth we realize from this is that faith is a blessing. Then what kind of blessing can faith specifically offer in our lives? The best answer is found in the confession of our forefathers of faith shown in Hebrews 11. We often call this chapter the "Chapter of Faith." It can be seen as the Hall of Fame of our ancestors of faith.

In the great Christian classic, *The Pilgrim's Progress*, Christian reaches House Beautiful where he takes a moment of rest in the chamber of peace. Then, he is ushered into the next room. In that room, he encounters the record of the ancestors of faith who went before him. Hebrews 11 is representative of these records. Through this chapter of faith, we can uncover the amazing truth that faith is a blessing. Why, then, is faith a blessing?

The Reason Faith is a Blessing

First, faith gives birth to great hope.

The great chapter of faith, Hebrews 11, begins as follows.

> "Faith is the reality of what we hope for, the proof of what we don't see" (Heb. 11:1, CEB).

The Hebrews author writes that faith is what we hope for, that is to say, the reality of what we hope for. The word "reality" used here in Greek is *upostasis* (under + stand) which signifies a foundation that strongly upholds something. This shows that faith is the foundation of hope. If one does not believe, hope is not a reality but an illusion. Faith is the reality of hope. At the same time, the verse states that faith is the evidence of what we do not see. The word "evidence" here can also be expressed as "deposit." Faith guarantees the certain future that we do not see.

Then why is our faith the foundation of confident hope and firm guarantee of our future? It is because our faith is based on the solid promise of God's Word. The ancients, our forefathers of faith, had experienced this truth(verse 2), and declared that our faith is connected to the Word of God(verse 3). Recall Romans 10:17:

> "Consequently, faith comes from hearing the message, and the message is heard through the word about Christ."

Let's take a look at how faith gave birth to such great hope through the lives of the forefathers that appear in Hebrews 11.

Abraham, the father of faith, originally lived each day without any hope, worshipping idols. However, one day, God appeared to him and said:

> "Go from your country, your people and your father's household to the land I will show you. "I will make you into a great nation, and I will bless you; I will make your name great, and you will be a

blessing" (Gen. 12:1-2).

Can you imagine how much hope this word must have given Abraham?

> "By faith Abraham, when called to go to a place he would later receive as his inheritance, obeyed and went, even though he did not know where he was going" (Heb. 11:8).

Although he had no knowledge or information about the new land, he left for the unknown territory in faith because it was God's word of promise. As a result, he eventually became the father of faith and progenitor of the chosen people. His name became Abraham ("the father of multitudes") from Abram ("exalted father").

Today, believers all around the world regard Abraham as the spiritual father. The moment he accepted the word of promise and believed, his hope of becoming the spiritual father of great nations became a concrete reality.

Think about Abraham's wife, Sarah. She received the word that God would give her the promised son, but when her menstruation ceased and her ability to reproduce failed, she lost her hope. Then God appeared to her again and said,

> "Is anything too hard for the LORD? I will return to you at the appointed time next year, and Sarah will have a son"(Gen. 18:14).

This was the very moment when her hope of becoming the mother of a great son was revived.

> "And by faith even Sarah, who was past childbearing age, was enabled to bear children because she considered him faithful who had made the promise"(Heb. 11:11).

What are the keywords that start this verse? They are "by faith." By faith, Sarah was able to bring back the flame of hope and give birth to the promised son, Isaac. Her name was also changed from Sara("queen") to Sarah("queen of all nations"). Faith, especially faith in the Word of God, is the foundation and deposit of great hope. Faith is truly a blessing. That is because only faith gives birth to great hope, as in the case of Abraham and Sarah.

Second, faith gives birth to great action.

The Korean Church is in a crisis due to the discrepancy between its faith and action. The actions of believers are disappointing the world. Many times, we see action separated from faith. So often, we are people of faith within the church, but the instance we go into the world, our actions do not testify to our faith. Our faith is valid only during the worship service and expires the moment we exit to the church parking lot. Have you seen believers arguing over trivial matters at the parking lot right after a worship service? There is a Christian joke that goes, "The church parking lot is where grace abounds the most." It is because so much grace is abandoned at the parking lot.

However, the truth is this. Sincere faith gives birth to sincere action. The real reason why one's action is not desirable is because their action is not based on faith. True faith and action are not separated because faith gives birth to action.

In *The Pilgrim's Progress*, Christian is led to a study where he comes across an ancient scroll containing the testimonies of Hebrews 11. Christian learns here about how the ancients put their faith into action in their lives. The following is a testimony of the so-called judges:

> "…who through faith conquered kingdoms, administered justice, and gained what was promised; who shut the mouths of lions, quenched the fury of the flames, and escaped the edge of the sword; whose weakness was turned to strength; and who became

powerful in battle and routed foreign armies" (Heb. 11:33-34).

Notice here the great actions born to faith. Faith and action do not contradict each other. Through faith they received courage that led to their front-line victory, and by faith they acted righteously. Faith gave birth to courage, and faith gave birth to acts of righteousness. If a person considers himself a man of faith but does not show it through his actions, then his faith is a false faith or a dead faith. Look at James's testimony in 2:26.

> "As the body without the spirit is dead, so faith without deeds is dead."

Third, faith gives the gift of salvation.
There can be many blessings that we experience after we put our faith in Jesus. But there is no greater blessing than salvation itself. The reason that Jesus came to earth was for this great salvation. The angel who prophesied His birth in the book of Matthew delivered the following word of prophecy.

> "She will give birth to a son, and you are to give him the name Jesus, because he will save his people from their sins" (Matt. 1:21).

The Hebrews author emphasizes the importance of salvation.

> "…how shall we escape if we ignore so great a salvation? This salvation, which was first announced by the Lord, was confirmed to us by those who heard him" (Heb. 2:3).

This verse uses the expression "great a salvation." We have received this great salvation through faith. The forefathers' experiences mentioned in Hebrews 11 testify to this.

Let's take a look at the case of Noah.

> "By faith Noah, when warned about things not yet seen, in holy fear built an ark to save his family. By his faith he condemned the world and became heir of the righteousness that is in keeping with faith" (Heb. 11:7).

It is said that because of the sins of that generation, God gave warning about the coming flood of judgment. He commanded Noah and the people of his generation to build an ark and enter it. However, only Noah and his family believed in God's Word, prepared and went inside the ark in faith, and were saved. There was no incident that was more important, more urgent, or greater during Noah's time than entering the ark and receiving salvation. It was an incident that signified the coming of Jesus as the ark of salvation for this generation. Even now, there is nothing more important than believing that Jesus Christ is the savior, abiding in Him, and receiving salvation. This is why the Bible tells us:

> "Believe in the Lord Jesus, and you will be saved—you and your household" (Acts 16:31).

Let's take another look into the Passover incident.

> "By faith he kept the Passover and the application of blood, so that the destroyer of the firstborn would not touch the firstborn of Israel" (Heb. 11:28).

On the night that God decided to judge Pharaoh and the land of Egypt by taking away the life of all firstborns, He decided to extend grace to houses that applied the blood of a young lamb on their doorposts as an atonement sacrifice.

> "When the Lord goes through the land to strike down the Egyptians, he will see the blood on the top and sides of the doorframe

and will pass over that doorway, and he will not permit the destroyer to enter your houses and strike you down"(Ex. 12:23).

Biblical scholar Arthur Pink says that there were most likely three types of people that night.

The first type of people did not think much of the blood and did not apply it on their doorposts. In other words, they were unbelievers who rejected God's way of salvation. What awaited them the next day was judgment, the death of their firstborns. Even today, the same judgment and destruction await our unbelieving neighbors who reject Jesus' cross and the shedding of His blood of atonement, God's way of salvation.

The second type of people are the ones who trusted in God's word and applied the blood of the lamb on the doorposts and the sides of their doors. It was the night of judgment, but these people of faith were able to praise the God of salvation until the approach of dawn. These people of faith greeted the new morning with thanksgiving and praise upon confirming that their firstborns were spared.

Finally, there was the third type of people. Even after applying the blood of the lamb on their doorposts, they were worried and anxious, staying up all night. Only when morning came and they saw that their firstborns were still alive did they finally let out a sigh of relief.

What is the issue with the third type of people? They indeed had enough faith to follow God's Word and apply the blood of the lamb on their doorposts. However, their faith was not enough to completely put their trust in Him and sleep soundly. This is why they spent the night in fear when they could have rested in peace. If you are going to believe, you need to believe wholeheartedly. Trust that faith is a blessing that provides not only great salvation but also assurance of salvation, peace, and a confident night's rest.

I pray for peace for all who have entered into the blessing of faith. Praise God who is the author and perfecter of our faith.

Questions for the Pilgrimage of Faith

1. Explain why faith is a blessing.

1)

2)

3)

2. Abraham and Sarah became people of hope when they put their trust in God's word. What can you do to reignite the flame of hope through faith?

3. Reflect on your faith and testify about the condition of your faith through Hebrews 11, the chapter of faith.

4. Our faith and actions can sometimes be different in our daily lives. In what instances is this the case? Why do you think our faith and actions do not match?

True faith and action are not separated

because faith gives birth to action.

Ephesians 6:10-13

Finally, be strong in the Lord and in his mighty power. Put on the full armor of God, so that you can take your stand against the devil's schemes. For our struggle is not against flesh and blood, but against the rulers, against the authorities, against the powers of this dark world and against the spiritual forces of evil in the heavenly realms. Therefore put on the full armor of God, so that when the day of evil comes, you may be able to stand your ground, and after you have done everything, to stand.

Pilgrim's Progress 16

Blessing of Putting On Spiritual Armor

A Lesson to Guard the Home

The Scripture that accounts the full armor recorded in Ephesians 6:10-13 in fact begins from Ephesians 5:22. Then what is the theme of the lesson that starts from Ephesians 5:22? In one word, it is the "home."

Ephesians 5:22 begins with "wives" and verse 25 with "husbands"(the Bible first calls the wives before the husbands to give the lesson). Then 6:1 calls on "children," and verse 4 calls on "fathers." Verse 5 calls on "bondservants" who were helpers in home ministry during those times, and verse 9 calls on "masters." The passage hereby delivers a lesson for each member to guard the home in their respective roles.

Today, homes are falling apart. We live in the "postmodern" era. The two words that describe this post-modern age are "destruction" and "dissolution." Many values and systems that were firmly maintained up until the "modern" age are now being destroyed and dismantled. The most significant destruction is happening in the home.

The Bible finds the cause for this phenomenon in spiritual reasons rather than mere psychological or ethical reasons. In Ephesians 6:12, Paul finds the fundamental reason behind the destruction of homes in "spiritual struggle," or to be more precise, "spiritual warfare." "For our struggle is not against flesh and blood, but against··· the spiritual forces of evil in the heavenly realms." Thus, in order to gain victory in this fight and guard our homes, we need to be spiritually armed.

> "Therefore put on the full armor of God, so that when the day of evil comes, you may be able to stand your ground, and after you have done everything, to stand" (Eph. 6:13).

Starting from verse 14, Apostle Paul lists in detail the weapons that the ancient warriors used in order to survive and protect themselves in battle.

In *The Pilgrim's Progress*, Christian reaches House Beautiful after climbing Hill Difficulty. There are three rooms at House Beautiful. The first room is the chamber of peace, the second room is the study, and the third is the armory. This shows that without being spiritually equipped, it is impossible to walk life's pilgrim road. At House Beautiful, Christian is armed from head to toe and then continues on his pilgrimage. Why do we need to be spiritually armed in our life pilgrimage?

Three Reasons that We Need to be Spiritually Armed on our Pilgrimage

First, it is to resist Satan's schemes.

> "Put on the full armor of God, so that you can take your stand against the devil's schemes" (Eph. 6:11).

To have victory in spiritual battle and protect our homes, we need to acknowledge the existence of the devil who seeks to destroy and break down our homes. In human history, the 17th and the 18h centuries are referred to as the age of Enlightenment. One of the most notable changes that happened during the Enlightenment era was the denial of the existence of the supernatural world and supernatural beings, which were universally acknowledged before.

Previously, people believed in a supernatural world and supernatural beings such as gods, angels, and devils although they were invisible. However, with the advancement of reason and science during the Enlightenment age, people came to believe that a world which could not be verified or scientifically proven did not exist. They believed that mankind could build a utopian world on this earth just by reason and science alone.

After the 19th century, however, humanity's reasoning and science brought calamity upon the earth by causing the First and Second World Wars. Thereafter, mankind finally realized that reason and science could not amount to everything, and their worldview started to change. One of the changes while entering the 20th century was that they started acknowledging again the existence of an invisible god and the devil. Eventually, man came to realize that we cannot make a better world without overcoming the evil nature within us. This is what has triggered the spiritual revival which began in the late 19th century and has continued into the 20th and the 21st centuries.

The word "devil" used in Ephesians 6:11 is *diabolos* in the original Greek. This word is a combination of two words, *dia*(between) and *bolos*(throw), which means coming into a relationship to break it apart(it is also translated as "slanderer").

Who is destroying marriages and breaking up relationships between parents and children? The devil is. The devil is using our inherent depravity to ruin the foundation of our lives. To resist the schemes of the devil, who is a spiritual being, simply being armed psychologically or morally is not enough. This is why we need to be spiritually armed.

Second, we can resist the devil only through the power of God.

> "Finally, be strong in the Lord and in his mighty power"(Eph. 6:10).

What preparation do we need in order to counter the devil who is a spiritual being? Apostle Paul tells us that we must stand firm in the Lord and be strong first in His mighty power.

The devil surpasses humans in many ways. A theologian in the past said, "The devil deserves several PhDs." The devil sees through the human heart and cleverly maneuvers it. He is a Doctor of Psychology. The devil reads the thought processes of humans and attempts to turn around ideologies. He is a Doctor of Philosophy. The devil comes into the world system, corrupting and incapacitating it. He is a Doctor of Political Science. The devil uses human hunger for power to trigger military arms and drives the world to warfare. He is a military strategist. The devil uses human greed for money to lead people to unceasing competition and makes them slaves to desire. He is a Doctor of Economics.

Take note that this verse is using the word "schemes" of the devil. "Scheme" comes from *methodoia*, the origin for the English word "method." The devil devises all sorts of plans, always plotting to intervene in our lives at his pleasure. According to the testimony in Genesis, the devil was cunning from the very beginning. Not only that, but as we can see in Ephesians 6:12, the devil moves in a well-organized, large-scaled, and systematically ordered manner.

> "For our struggle is not against flesh and blood, but against the rulers, against the authorities, against the powers of this dark world

and against the spiritual forces of evil in the heavenly realms."

Here the "rulers" and "authorities," "powers of this dark world" and "spiritual forces of evil in the heavenly realms" show the collectivity of evil spirits at work in different areas that are all under the rule of the devil. These refer to spirits that are at work in ruling the world, spirits that work behind the huge natural powers, spirits that instigate rulers of the world to stir up things of the dark world, and spirits that work in heavenly realms apart from the earth.

Like a massive military organization, they are at work on the earth and in the heavenly realms. It is impossible for a mere believer to fight and win against such spiritual organization with their own strength. In Eugene Peterson's *The Message*, the verses following Ephesians 6:12 are written as follows.

> "This is for keeps, a life-or-death fight to the finish against the Devil and all his angels. Be prepared. You're up against far more than you can handle on your own."

In spite of this, there is good news that we need to remember. Although the devil acts based on a vast amount of information, he is not all-knowing. He may be more powerful than man, but he is not all-powerful.

Only our Lord God and His Son Jesus Christ are omnipotent and omniscient. Therefore, as long as we remain in the Lord and rely on His power, we need not fear the devil or his evil spirits. Scripture tells us to "be strong in the Lord and in His mighty power."

Third, being spiritually armed is the first step to being prepared for spiritual warfare.

You cannot expect victory in war if the soldiers are unprepared or unarmed. Therefore, Paul first directs us to be spiritually equipped in order to gain victory in the spiritual warfare that is to happen. "Therefore put on the full armor of God" (verse 13). Continuing in verse 14 and the following verses, the actual form of the spiritual armor is presented. If we take a closer look, we see that there are five weapons for defense and two for offense.

The first defensive weapon is the "belt of truth." Belts help to hold up one's posture. It must be buckled up correctly in order to give strength. "Stand firm then with the belt of truth buckled around your waist" (verse 14). Believing in the truth and standing firm is the first priority.

The second defensive weapon is the "breastplate of righteousness." We need to be dressed with the righteousness of Jesus to guard our hearts.

The third defensive weapon is the "feet fitted with the gospel of peace." Shoes need to be comfortable in order for one to walk and run well in them. We must be ready to go anywhere at any time with the feet fitted with the gospel of peace.

The fourth defensive weapon is the "shield of faith." Only an unwavering trust in God can extinguish the flaming arrows of the evil one.

The fifth defensive weapon is the "helmet of salvation." This weapon is to protect the brain which is crucial for survival. Assurance of salvation and hope are the most powerful weapons that protect us.

Apostle Paul goes on to list the two offensive weapons. They are the "Word" and "prayer." We have no chance for victory in spiritual warfare without the Word and prayer. Apostle Paul refers to the Word as the "sword of the Spirit." When we stay close to God's Word, meditate on it, and arm ourselves with the Word, the Spirit enables us to overpower the devil and gain victory using the Word within us. However, being armed with the Word does not complete the spiritual armor just yet. Prayer for all things is necessary.

> "And pray in the Spirit on all occasions with all kinds of prayers

and requests. With this in mind, be alert and always keep on praying for all the Lord's people" (Eph. 6:18).

In one verse, the word "all" in English, *pas* or *panta* in Greek, is mentioned five times: "all kinds of prayers and requests," "always keep on praying"(all occasions), and "all the Lord's people." Prayer is an "all court pressing" weapon that defeats the devil. Eugene Peterson writes this verse in *The Message* as follows.

> "God's Word is an indispensable weapon. In the same way, prayer is essential in this ongoing warfare. Pray hard and long. Pray for your brothers and sisters. Keep your eyes open. Keep each other's spirits up so that no one falls behind or drops out."

In *The Pilgrim's Progress*, Christian boldly sets out on his pilgrimage after receiving newfound strength and being equipped with the full armor of God from the armory at House Beautiful.

In our earthly pilgrimage, we have two House Beautifuls. They are the "church" and the "home." Only the homes that have been properly equipped with spiritual armor through the church can resist the devil's attack. The biggest blessing the church can give is providing spiritual armor. Sunday sermons alone are not enough.

Various kinds of training, teaching programs, and discipleship training provided at church are opportunities for us to be spiritually armed.

Arise as God's mighty soldier through the spiritual armor. Stand up in Jesus' name. Be equipped with the Lord-given power and go out to the valley that is awaiting us. Though the enemy approaches, we will not fall.

Questions for the Pilgrimage of Faith

1. What does the Bible say is the fundamental cause behind the destruction and breakdown of homes? What needs to be done to guard our homes?

2. List three reasons why believers need to be spiritually armed:
1)
2)
3)

3. Which spiritual weapon do you especially need these days?

4. The full armor of God consists of five defensive weapons and two offensive weapons. Explain each weapon and reflect on the meaning of each one.

Only our Lord God and His Son Jesus Christ are
omnipotent and omniscient.
Therefore, as long as we remain in the Lord
and rely on His power,
we need not fear the devil or his evil spirits.

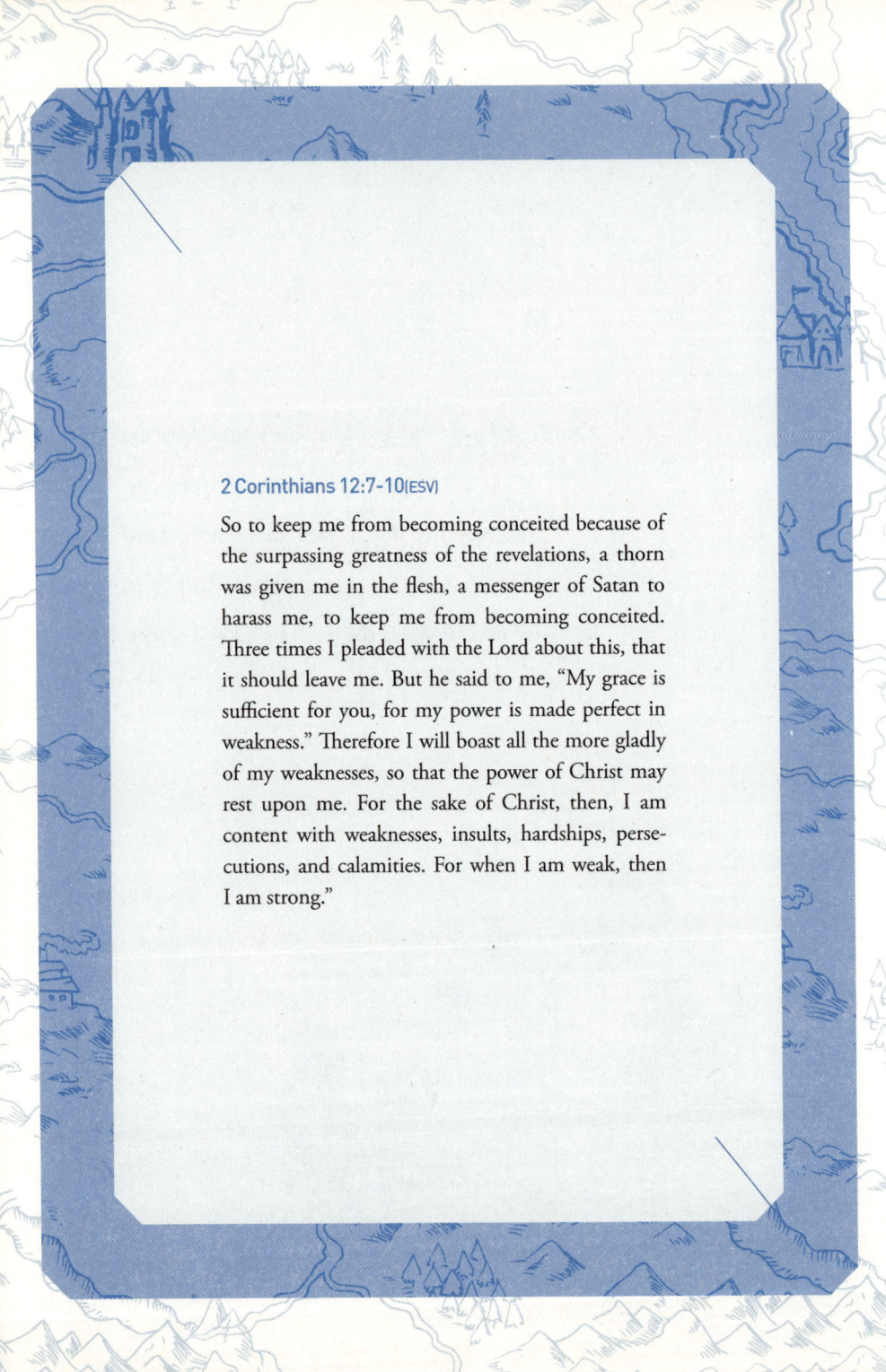

2 Corinthians 12:7-10 (ESV)

So to keep me from becoming conceited because of the surpassing greatness of the revelations, a thorn was given me in the flesh, a messenger of Satan to harass me, to keep me from becoming conceited. Three times I pleaded with the Lord about this, that it should leave me. But he said to me, "My grace is sufficient for you, for my power is made perfect in weakness." Therefore I will boast all the more gladly of my weaknesses, so that the power of Christ may rest upon me. For the sake of Christ, then, I am content with weaknesses, insults, hardships, persecutions, and calamities. For when I am weak, then I am strong."

Pilgrim's Progress 17

Valley of Humiliation

When You Encounter the Valleys of Life

Jane Eggleston, a believer, wrote a poem titled "It's In The Valley I Grow."

> "Sometimes life seems hard to bear,
> Full of sorrow, trouble and woe.
> It's then I have to remember
> That it's in the valleys I grow.

If I always stayed on the mountain top

And never experienced pain,

I would never appreciate God's love

And would be living in vain.

I have so much to learn

And my growth is very slow.

Sometimes I need the mountain tops,

But it's in the valleys I grow."

When we look back on life, there are times when we feel as if we have passed through a valley. In *The Pilgrim's Progress*, Christian experiences peace and rest at House Beautiful, learns faith from the forefathers of faith, and arms himself spiritually. He continues his walk after receiving a loaf of bread, a bottle of wine, and a cluster of raisins as the House Beautiful family sees him off.

What awaits Christian not long after, however, is the Valley of Humiliation that leads downward. Immediately after he steps into the valley, he is faced with the monster Apollyon. Apollyon is a being mentioned in Revelations 9:11.

"They had as king over them the angel of the Abyss, whose name in

Hebrew is Abaddon, and in Greek, Apollyon(that is, Destroyer)."

John Bunyan describes Apollyon as a monster covered with scales like a fish and wings like a dragon. The monster, which is the devil, throws flaming darts at Christian as though he is pouring hail upon him. Using his shield, Christian resists with all his might but ends up getting injured in the head, hands, and feet.

In 2 Corinthians, Apostle Paul confesses that in his life pilgrimage, he was also wounded by Satan's flaming darts.

> "So to keep me from becoming conceited because of the surpassing greatness of the revelations, a thorn was given me in the flesh, a messenger of Satan to harass me, to keep me from becoming conceited" (2 Cor. 12:7, ESV).

Apostle Paul says that Satan harassed him, and as a result he experienced pain from the thorn in his flesh. Apostle Paul says that the pain is from the messenger of Satan.

We do not know exactly what this thorn is. Some scholars assume that Apostle Paul was suffering from an incurable disease such as an eye problem or epilepsy. Other scholars state that when Apostle Paul was living life as a missionary after his conversion, the legalists that tormented and persecuted him acted as messengers of Satan and tortured him throughout his whole life. Whether it was from a disease or people, Apostle Paul had a painful thorn from Satan's attacks.

How do you think Apostle Paul treated the thorn in his life? In order to walk on life's pilgrimage road that God purposed for us, we must realize the true meaning of the thorns in our lives and have a clear stance on them.

Stance on Life's Thorns

First, life's thorns are God's gift.

Surprisingly, Apostle Paul rejoices and gives thanks to God for his thorn, rather than complaining about it.

> "For the sake of Christ, then, I am content with weaknesses, insults, hardships, persecutions, and calamities. For when I am weak, then I am strong" (2 Cor. 12:10, ESV).

It is a praise of joy and gratitude. How is this possible? Of course, as Apostle Paul is also human, he confesses in verse 8 that he prayed that the thorn would be taken away from him. He earnestly pleaded three times. However, in verse 9, the answer he received was not the disappearance of the thorn but the following words from God: "My grace is sufficient for you, for my power is made perfect in weakness."

Upon receiving these words, he rejoices greatly and says that he will boast about his weaknesses from then on. He chooses to be thankful. This is the famous "gratitude for the thorn" of Apostle Paul, the gratitude that he learned from life's valleys.

Christian from *The Pilgrim's Progress* also gives thanks in the same way. He is injured by Apollyon the destroyer. However, at a critical moment, Christian asks for God's help, and with His help he thrusts his sword, finally defeating Apollyon. In the next moment, Christian praises God, overflowing with joy. It is a praise of thankfulness.

> "Great Satan, the captain of this fiend,
> Designed my ruin; therefore to this end
> He sent him harnessed out: and he with rage
> That hellish was, did fiercely me engage;
> But blessed angels helped me; and I,
> By dint of sword, did quickly make him fly:

> Therefore to God let me give lasting praise,
>
> And thank and bless His holy name always."

It is in the valley that Christian gives thanks, the Valley of Humiliation. He learns here that victory depends on God's power, not his own strength.

Second, all believers must pass through the Valley of Humiliation.

Let us meditate on Apostle Paul's gratitude for the thorn. The greatest reason for his gratitude was that he learned humility through the thorn. Apostle Paul repeats twice in verse 7 that God placed the thorn to keep him "from being conceited."

There was nothing he could not do because of the thorn. Prayer did not take away the thorn, but he gained strength amidst weakness. Through the power of God that sustained him, he traveled around the world that was known to him a total of three times. He preached the gospel as he went, planted churches, and was used by God in His amazing work to change the world. He prayed more because of the thorn and leaned on God's power more because of it. Apostle Paul was able to live as a warrior for the gospel because the grace of Christ that overpowered the thorn was with him every step. The Valley of Humiliation he went through led him to experience God's grace.

What would have happened if Apostle Paul did not have this thorn? He would have been tempted by pride to elevate himself like God because of the many great revelations he received. If he had become prideful, he would have become a slave of Satan from that very moment. This is because Satan was originally a beautiful angel("Your heart became proud on account of your beauty" - Ezek. 28:17), and was thrown out of heaven because of his pride. Let us look at Isaiah 14:13-14 that points out how the archangel was corrupted.

> "You said in your heart, 'I will ascend to heaven; I will raise my throne above the stars of God; I will sit enthroned on the mount of assembly, on the utmost heights of Mount Zaphon. I will ascend above the tops of the clouds; I will make myself like the Most High.'"

There is a word that the evil one repeatedly emphasizes, almost like a spell: "I." He repeats "I" five times. Remember that when the word "I" is repeated with our lips, we are no longer slaves of God but slaves of Satan. On the other hand, when the word "God" or "Christ" comes out of our mouth, it proves that we are God's slaves, Christ's slaves.

At times in our life pilgrimage, God makes us pass through the low, downhill valley. He gives us wounds that are not fatal but make us cry out for God's help so that we learn humility. Therefore, life's trials are the Valleys of Humiliation that help us experience grace. When we pass through the Valley of Humiliation, we learn to not only be thankful for the rose but for its thorns, too.

Third, we can grow even in the valley.

August Ludvig Storm met Christ and was saved at a Salvation Army meeting when he was 29. Moved by the grace of salvation, he came home and wrote a poem. Eight years later, when he was 37, he started to feel pain in his back and was soon paralyzed on one side. Although he had physical disabilities, he devoted his lifetime as a minister of the gospel and became a minister for the Salvation Army. He lived for 15 more years as a powerful preacher, leading many souls to Jesus.

Storm said that the poem he wrote right after he met Jesus became a prophetic testimony of his life. The poem is the gospel hymn "Thanks to God."

"Thanks to God for my Redeemer,

Thanks for all Thou dost provide!

Thanks for times now but a mem'ry,

Thanks for Jesus by my side!

Thanks for pleasant, balmy springtime,

Thanks for dark and stormy fall!

Thanks for tears by now forgotten,

Thanks for peace within my soul!(verse 1)

Thanks for prayers that Thou hast answered,

Thanks for what Thou dost deny!

Thanks for storms that I have weathered,

Thanks for all Thou dost supply!

Thanks for pain, and thanks for pleasure,

Thanks for comfort in despair!

Thanks for grace that none can measure,

Thanks for love beyond compare!(verse 2)

Thanks for roses by the wayside,

Thanks for thorns their stems contain!

Thanks for home and thanks for fireside,

Thanks for hope, that sweet refrain!

Thanks for joy and thanks for sorrow,

Thanks for heav'nly peace with Thee!

Thanks for hope in the tomorrow,

Thanks through all eternity!(verse 3)"

The writer of this hymn wrote the poem through the guidance of the Holy Spirit, not knowing its true meaning. It was while he passed through life's valley, the Valley of Humiliation, that he learned the true meaning of the lyrics and what true gratitude means.

I shared Jane Eggleston's poem, "It's in the Valleys I Grow," in the beginning of the chapter. This is the last part of the poem.

> "Forgive me Lord, for complaining
> When I'm feeling so very low.
> Just give me a gentle reminder
> That it's in the valleys I grow.
>
> Continue to strengthen me, Lord
> And use my life each day
> To share your love with others
> And help them find their way.
>
> Thank you for valleys, Lord
> For this one thing I know.

> The mountain tops are glorious
>
> But it's in the valleys I grow!"

We must pray that we will learn to be thankful in the valleys of life, even in the valleys that wound us. In *The Pilgrim's Progress*, when Christian gives thanks, God's angel takes the leaves from the Tree of Life in heaven and applies it to his wounds. All the wounds are healed immediately. Christian gives thanks again, eats the bread, and drinks the wine. This is to remember that the source of our thankfulness is the body and blood of Jesus Christ who was sacrificed on the cross. I pray that we, too, will learn true thanksgiving day by day.

Questions for the Pilgrimage of Faith

1. What is the biggest lesson to take home from the Valley of Humiliation in our lives?

2. What is the reason that God allows us thorns?

3. Share and pray about the thorns that humble you today.

4. Write your own praise poem thanking God in spite of your circumstances.

At times, in our life pilgrimage,
God makes us pass through the low, downhill valley.
He gives us wounds that are not fatal
but make us cry out for God's help
so that we learn humility.

Psalm 23:4(ESV)

Even though I walk through the valley of the shadow of death, I will fear no evil, for you are with me; your rod and your staff, they comfort me.

Pilgrim's Progress 18

Valley of the Shadow of Death

Should You Meet the Shadow of Death in Life

A college student took an exam and received an F. Confounded, he went to his professor and said, "Professor, I know I didn't do a good job on the test, but I did try my best. I don't think I deserve an F."

The professor smiled and answered, "I also don't think that you deserve an F. But F is the lowest grade I can give. I couldn't give you a lower grade even if I wanted to."

What idiom could we use to describe this situation? How about "out of the frying-pan into the fire?" Bad things do not come one at a time.

In *The Pilgrim's Progress*, Christian finally makes his way out of the Valley of Humiliation after being wounded while defeating the devil Apollyon. However, another valley awaits him. It is the Valley of the Shadow of Death.

At the entrance of the Valley of the Shadow of Death, he runs into two men. They tell him not to even think about passing through the valley for the valley is pitch-black, filled with dragons and monsters, and sounds of wailing and moaning. They tell him to go back as they are if he wants to save his life.

Is this situation not like going "out of the frying-pan into the fire?" In our pilgrimage of life, painful situations like these can continue to torment us. After finally solving one problem, a bigger problem awaits us. Although these difficulties are not death itself, but just shadows, they make us feel death. "The shadow of death" mentioned in Psalm 23 originates from the word *tzalamut*, a combination of *tzal* and *mavet*, meaning "the shade or shadow of death." The King James Version translates this as the "shadow of death," which is also reflected in the Korean translation.

As we live our lives, even when we do not face death itself, we do experience the shadow of death. Don't we feel the shadow of death nearing us when we experience the loss of our close neighbors or unexpected diseases and accidents? We think, "Oh, I could die like this, too," rather than "Oh, fortunately I'm alive." Yes, we must all pass through the Valley of the Shadow of Death, with no exception. There is no other way to heaven than through this valley.

Yet, the gospel lies here. We must remember that Christian had three weapons that allow him to make his way through the Valley of the Shadow of Death.

Weapons Needed in the Valley of Death

The first weapon is "All-Prayer."
In *The Pilgrim's Progress*, a great amount of flames and smoke are gushing out from the entrance of the valley. Christian realizes that he cannot fight with his sword alone as with Apollyon in the Valley of Humiliation. He ponders for a while, then places the sword back in its sheath and decides to take out a different weapon. It is a new weapon called "All-prayer." He takes out this weapon and cries out, "O Lord I beseech Thee, deliver my soul." All-prayer is the ultimate offensive weapon of the spiritual armor that Apostle

Paul mentions in Ephesians 6.

> "And pray in the Spirit on all occasions with all kinds of prayers and requests. With this in mind, be alert and always keep on praying for all the Lord's people" (Eph. 6:18).

In prayer, Christian enters the valley that is filled with flames and smoke. Whenever fear comes upon him, he cries out in prayer, "I will walk in the strength of the Lord God." Then, the demons disappear.

What does it mean to pray? It means to depend on the Almighty God because we cannot depend on our own strength. Prayer connects us to the Almighty One. Then what does All-prayer mean? It is to go before God with all possible kinds of prayer. Pray in public. Pray in private. Pray out loud. Pray in silence. Pray for a long time. Pray for a short time. Pray early in the morning. Pray during the day and at night. Pray with your family. Pray at work and on the streets. Pray always. Pray with petitions. Pray with confessions. Pray with thanksgiving. Pray with praises.

The most important thing in prayer is to pray in the Holy Spirit. Let the Spirit lead the prayer. Sometimes, we might start praying without having the heart of prayer. It is better, however, than not praying at all.

When we desperately seek the Holy Spirit's help from the bottom of our hearts, we experience the Holy Spirit leading our prayer instead of us praying against our will. I believe that this is what happens when we pray in the Spirit. Does not all fear and worry disappear? We are finally able to rise up, captured by God's power which we receive when we pray. I hope that all of us can experience this kind of prayer and pass through the Valley of the Shadow of Death with All-prayer.

The second weapon is the "promise verse."

As Christian anxiously walks in the Valley of the Shadow of Death, he hears the voice of someone going before him. It is none other than Psalm 23:4.

> "Even though I walk through the valley of the shadow of death, I will fear no evil, for you are with me; your rod and your staff, they comfort me."

Christian calls to him, imagining someone meditating on the verse. However, the man repeats this verse instead of answering him. Christian continuously recites this verse as he walks. Suddenly, he realizes that the God who is with the pilgrim walking ahead of him is also with him. All fear is gone, and amazing peace comes upon him. Soon the valley is coming to an end and the day is breaking. Christian shouts for joy, "He hath turned the shadow of death into the morning."

A promise verse is like a lamp that those who are walking through valleys in life can trust more than anything else. Recall Psalm 119:105.

"Your word is a lamp to my feet, a light on my path."

Now let's hear Peter's testimony:

"We also have the prophetic message as something completely reliable, and you will do well to pay attention to it, as to a light shining in a dark place, until the day dawns and the morning star rises in your hearts" (2 Pet. 1:19).

In life's pilgrimage, sometimes the proverbs of wise men and the asceticism of saints can be of help. Church traditions and ceremonies can also assist a pilgrim's walk. However, there is a profound truth that the reformers discovered as they started reading the Bible. It is that there is no other light of truth more certain and clear than Scripture. This is why one of the slogans of the Reformation was "Sola Scriptura."

In *The Pilgrim's Progress*, Christian discovers an old pope and a dead pagan in a cave just as he is nearing the end of the valley. John Bunyan concluded that the pope, the spiritual leader who was misleading the Church at the time(the Puritan age), was like an old giant and that his existence was no different than that of a dead pagan. He was illustrating that a religious leader is not the one we should place our trust in.

This also applies to today's Christian leaders and pastors. Man can always become corrupt and go astray. This also includes the church. Therefore, we must go on the pilgrimage holding onto "Sola Scriptura," God's Word of promise alone. This is the true spirit of reformation.

The weapon that allows us to pass through the Valley of the Shadow of Death without being shaken is God's promises. Keep close to the Word. Study it and meditate on it. Live a life of obedience to the Word.

The third weapon is the "praise of victory."
After having come out of the valley safely, Christian sings praises.

"O, world of wonders! (I can say no less),

That I should be preserved in that distress

That I have met with here! Oh, blessed be

That hand that from it hath delivered me!

Dangers in darkness, devils, hell, and sin,

Did compass me, while I this vale was in;

Yes, snares, and pits, and traps, and nets did lie

My path about, that worthless, silly I

Might have been catched, entangled, and cast down;

But, since I live, let Jesus wear the crown."

From of old, our fathers in faith would confess, "Prayer helps us endure in spiritual battle, but praise ends the battle."

Apostle Paul changed the course of his missionary journey from Asia to Macedonia through the guidance of the Holy Spirit. While evangelizing in Philippi, the first city he visited in Macedonia, he healed a demon-possessed slave who was a fortune-teller. In fury that their source of income was gone, her masters accused Apostle Paul and Silas, and they were thrown into prison. After being severely beaten and chained with shackles, Apostle Paul and Silas sang praises to God that night.

In such situations, it is natural to complain. How can anyone sing praises? Is it not normal to say, "God, I came over to this land to be a witness of the gospel, and I suffered greatly because of you. But why this prison, this flogging, and these shackles?" But Apostle Paul praised God.

Why is this? It is because Apostle Paul believed in God's sovereignty. He was thankful to be given an opportunity to testify to the gospel, to suffer for the Lord, and for what was going to happen in the prison. Romans 8:28 says, "And we know that in all things God works for the good of those who love him, who have been called according to his purpose." Apostle Paul believed that God could work even trials like imprisonment for good. Therefore, he was able to praise Him.

What happened next? There was an earthquake and the prison doors flew open. Apostle Paul shared the gospel with the jailer, and the jailer and his whole family were saved. The door to missions in Philippi was wide open. That is why Scripture tells us to "give thanks in all circumstances"(1 Thess. 5:18). If we change this verse a little bit, it can be: "give praise in all circumstances."

There was a man who healed many souls by testifying about being thankful in all circumstances and preaching on only one subject: the power of praise. He was an American army chaplain named Merlin R. Carothers.

A young man named Jim listened to his preaching and told his wife, "For many years, we have been praying that my alcoholic father would change, but I don't think we have been thankful for God's providence in this situation. Let's give thanks from now on."

His wife retorted, "How can we be thankful?" Jim answered, "Don't we believe in God who works everything for our good?" He then shared what he heard from Rev. Merlin Carothers. From that day forward, every time they thought of their father, the couple thanked God for him and praised God for what He would do in his life.

The next Sunday, their father asked them out of the blue, "If someone like me believes in Jesus, can they be saved from alcoholism?"

In a few weeks' time, Jim's father received Jesus and was freed from alcoholism.

This is the power of praise. Rev. Merlin Carothers says, "If we start to live our lives trusting, praising and thanking God, God will fight our battles for us from that very moment."

Indeed, praise that believes in God's victory is a gift from heaven that helps us pass through the Valley of the Shadow of Death. Praise God now.

Questions for the Pilgrimage of Faith

1. What are the three weapons that we need in order to pass through the Valley of the Shadow of Death?
1)
2)
3)

2. What is the weapon that you need the most?

3. What is the prayer that conquers all fear and worry?

4. Have you experienced the power of praise? If so, share your experience in detail.

1 Corinthians 4:15-21

Even if you had ten thousand guardians in Christ, you do not have many fathers, for in Christ Jesus I became your father through the gospel. Therefore I urge you to imitate me. For this reason I have sent to you Timothy, my son whom I love, who is faithful in the Lord. He will remind you of my way of life in Christ Jesus, which agrees with what I teach everywhere in every church. Some of you have become arrogant, as if I were not coming to you. But I will come to you very soon, if the Lord is willing, and then I will find out not only how these arrogant people are talking, but what power they have. For the kingdom of God is not a matter of talk but of power. What do you prefer? Shall I come to you with a rod of discipline, or shall I come in love and with a gentle spirit?

Pilgrim's Progress 19

Faithful and Talkative

A True Worker and a Slick Talker

Our ancestors used to say that children who learn well in the village schools(the educational institution of Korea's past) become "faithful workers," and those who do not become "slick talkers." Both faithful workers and slick talkers were educated in the same room. This is also the case for a spiritual community. Among those who walk the path of faith, there are true workers, but also those who are simply big talkers.

In his letters to the Corinthian church, Paul mentions that there are true workers and slick talkers among the people he met.

First, Apostle Paul chooses Timothy, his disciple and ministry successor, as a model of a true worker. In 1 Corinthians 4:17, Timothy is described as Paul's beloved son, "faithful to the Lord." He goes on, however, to say that there are people in the Corinthian church who are arrogant, who are only talkative and not living a powerful life worthy of Scripture. They were not workers, but talkers. Apostle Paul tells them,

"For the kingdom of God is not a matter of talk but of power"(1 Cor. 4:20).

John Bunyan calls these two types of people Faithful and Talkative.

Around the time Christian comes out of the Valley of the Shadow of Death, he finds a man who is walking ahead of him with unshaken and consistent footsteps. He is Faithful, a trustworthy man whose very sight made him desirable as a companion.

Unable to catch up to him easily, Christian runs to him. Finally, they start walking together, shoulder to shoulder. Companionship with Faithful, how desirable is that? His experiences in faith and his testimonies that he shares are greatly encouraging. Christian is strengthened as he hears how Faithful overcame the temptation of Wanton, his encounter with Adam the First and his three Daughters, the Lust of the Flesh, the Lust of the Eyes, and the Pride of Life, how he met Discontent and Shame, and finally how he thwarted all temptations and got out of the Valley of the Shadow of Death. This testifies to the benefits of having good companionship.

However, in our path of faith, we do not only meet faithful people. Soon after, Christian and Faithful encounter a tall and attractive man, Talkative.

This shows the two contrasting images of pilgrims that we meet on our pilgrimage. Depending on whom we spend more time with, we reach different levels of spiritual maturity. Thus, we need to look closely into the two contrasting forms of pilgrims.

The Two Kinds of Pilgrims We Meet on Our Pilgrimage

First, the pilgrim we should walk with is Faithful.
In *The Pilgrim's Progress*, John Bunyan describes Faithful as someone who overcomes temptations and walks on the path of faith,

unshaken and constant. Furthermore, he is portrayed as being edifying and having a good influence on others.

Then, what kind of person was Timothy, whom Apostle Paul describes as a son "faithful to the Lord?" To Paul, Timothy was a disciple more trustworthy than anyone else, the one who could take his place in his absence. He had encouraged Timothy early on as follows:

> "Don't let anyone look down on you because you are young, but set an example for the believers in speech, in life, in love, in faith and in purity" (1 Tim. 4:12).

In other words, he is encouraging Timothy to become someone who is trustworthy in speech, in life, in love, in faith, and in purity. All of this stated in one word is faithfulness.

In 1 Timothy 4:15, Apostle Paul says, "give yourself wholly to them, so that everyone may see your progress." Timothy proved his faithful progress by reaching maturity, which was evident to his neighbors. That is why Apostle Paul sent Timothy, whom he trusted most, on his behalf whenever problems arose within the Corinthian church.

This was not only so for the Corinthian church. When Apostle

Paul wanted to teach the Philippi church members through his letters, the first person he thought of was Timothy.

> "I hope in the Lord Jesus to send Timothy to you soon, that I also may be cheered when I receive news about you. I have no one else like him, who takes a genuine interest in your welfare"(Phil. 2:19-20).

We can see Timothy's faithfulness once more in the expression "who takes a genuine interest in your welfare." However, we need to note that this faithfulness was not something Timothy had in his nature, but rather a fruit of spiritual discipline.

> "For everyone looks out for his own interests, not those of Jesus Christ. But you know that Timothy has proved himself, because as a son with his father he has served with me in the work of the gospel"(Phil. 2:21-22).

Let us pay attention to the expression "proved himself." Apostle Paul says that Timothy's faithfulness was the fruit of his service to the gospel. Who would believe in the gospel if it is testified by the lips of an unfaithful person? Those who want to live as witnesses to the gospel are first tested for their faithfulness.

God grants favor not only to believers but also to non-believers. Theologians call this "common grace." That is how in many cases unbelievers have more talents and gifts than we do. However, there is one character trait that believers should never fall short of in comparison to unbelievers, and that is faithfulness. It is because faithfulness is the most important attribute of God. The reason why we must live faithfully is that the God we believe in and depend on is faithful.

> "Know therefore that the Lord your God is God; he is the faithful God, keeping his covenant of love to a thousand generations of those who love him and keep his commands" (Deut. 7:9).

This is a testimony that remains unchanged even in the New Testament era.

> "God, who has called you into fellowship with his Son Jesus Christ our Lord, is faithful" (1 Cor. 1:9).

Our Faithful God who has called His covenant people and made them His faithful disciples wants to use them as a light for this generation that has lost faithfulness.

Second, the pilgrim we should avoid is Talkative.

We influence and are influenced by those around us. This is why a saying in the west goes, "Show me your friends, and I'll tell you who you are." Your life companions are so important.

What kind of person was Talkative, whom Christian met on his way to heaven? Christian discloses Talkative's identity to Faithful as the following:

"Notwithstanding his fine tongue, he is but a sorry fellow."

In other words, he is someone whose words and actions do not match. As the soul and body are separate, his faith and actions are separate. He does not pray and has never repented for his sins with a sincere heart. He speaks angelic words like a sounding gong, but has no love. In many cases he easily deceives people into thinking that he is a devout believer with his words.

In this passage, John Bunyan quotes two verses:

> "So you must obey them and do everything they tell you. But do not do what they do, for they do not practice what they preach"(Matt. 23:3).

The people that this quoted verse is targeting are the Pharisees of Jesus' time. The Pharisees quoted Scripture well and boasted of their knowledge of the Torah. However, there was no evidence that they were living according to the Word.

In the following verse, he points out those who do not live out God's Kingdom.

> "For the kingdom of God is not a matter of talk but of power" (1 Cor. 4:20).

Who were they? 1 Corinthians chapter 1 onwards shows us that they divided the Corinthian church. They were talkers without any devotion or action, and they were breaking the love in the church community by planting doubt about Apostle Paul's apostleship.

The "power" that Apostle Paul mentions here does not indicate supernatural gifts or signs. It signifies the "power of life" to live out the Word. When Christian points out to Talkative that he is lacking in this power, Talkative stops talking and leaves their fellowship. When he disappears, Faithful praises God.

> "How Talkative at first lifts up his plumes!
> How bravely doth he speak! How he presumes
> To drive down all before him! But so soon

As Faithful talks of heart-work, like the moon

That's past the full, into the wane he goes;

And so will all but he who heart-work knows."

These people refuse a change of heart. Truth is on their lips, but it does not govern their hearts. We cannot expect from them sincere devotion where truth becomes their hands and feet. The Word does not become flesh in them. In one word, they are unfaithful.

What is interesting is that when we write "faithful"(信實) or "sincere"(誠實) in Chinese characters, the letter indicating "word"(言) is used. The first half of the word "faithful" is a combination of the Chinese characters for "man"(亻) and "word"(言). And the second half of the word(實) means fruit. Therefore, "faithful"(信實) is the fruit of one's word. Likewise, the first half of the word "sincere" is a combination of the Chinese characters for "word"(言) and "fulfill"(成). The second half of the word "sincere"(實) also means fruit. "Sincerity"(誠實) is a fruit that comes from fulfilling one's word. Our generation needs sincere witnesses who hold onto and live out the Word, rain or shine, in the springtime or summertime.

There was a man born in a cottage in a small Kentucky town who had a dream of becoming a teacher. His family situation was so poor that he could not get a proper education. So he taught himself and finally became a teacher. However, having been weak from a young age, he had to quit his teaching job due to health issues.

Later when he became 27, he attended a revival meeting where he was blessed and started dreaming to be a pastor who shares the gospel. When he was 36, he finally became a Methodist minister. However, due to health issues again, he had to give up his position as a pastor within one year. With no other choices, he became an insurance planner since this job did not require of him regular work hours.

Having quit his job as a teacher and then a pastor, he received many glares from his relatives and neighbors. However, he experienced a great blessing one day as he was meditating on Lamentations at home.

> "Because of the Lord's great love we are not consumed, for his compassions never fail. They are new every morning; great is your faithfulness" (Lam. 3:22-23).

He realized that although he had to give up on his dreams of becoming a teacher and a pastor due to health problems, it was by God's faithful grace that he was able to live each day with his family. He could take care of his health as an insurance planner, and although not on a podium, he could share the gospel with the people he met.

With a thankful heart, he took a pen and wrote a poem. This is "Great is Thy Faithfulness," the hymn of the century by Thomas Chisholm.

> "Great is Thy faithfulness, O God my Father
> There is no shadow of turning with Thee
> Thou changest not, Thy compassions they fail not
> As Thou hast been, Thou forever wilt be.(Verse 1)
> Summer and winter and springtime and harvest
> Sun, moon, and stars in their courses above
> Join with all nature in manifold witness
> To Thy great faithfulness, mercy, and love.(Verse 2)
> Great is Thy faithfulness
> Great is Thy faithfulness
> Morning by morning new mercies I see
> All I have needed Thy hand hath provided
> Great is Thy faithfulness, Lord unto me.(Chorus)"

Are we living today by God's faithful grace? If so, I pray that we would reveal through our lives that we are the children of a faithful God by worshipping Him, having fellowship with faithful believers, and building a godly, faithful character.

Questions for the Pilgrimage of Faith

1. What are the two contrasting types of pilgrims that we meet on our pilgrimage of faith?

1)

2)

2. Who are the figures in the Bible that represent the two groups? Share the traits of each.

3. Share what the essence of biblical faithfulness is.

4. What can we do to reveal that we are children of a faithful God in our everyday lives?

Ecclesiastes 1:1-2

The words of the Teacher, son of David, king in Jerusalem: "Meaningless! Meaningless!" says the Teacher. "Utterly meaningless! Everything is meaningless."

Ecclesiastes 12:13-14

Now all has been heard; here is the conclusion of the matter: Fear God and keep his commandments, for this is the duty of all mankind. For God will bring every deed into judgment, including every hidden thing, whether it is good or evil.

Pilgrim's Progress 20

Vanity Fair

Vanity Fair, the Essence of a Wordly Life

Most people wander in life because they do not know that the essence of the world is a Vanity Fair. This is why John Bunyan places Vanity Fair as a place that Christian must go through. Pilgrims encounter this village at the end of the wilderness, and cannot avoid going through the always open fair. Let us think upon the three lessons that Vanity Fair teaches us.

The Three Lessons Vanity Fair Teaches Us

First, all pursuits of this world are in vain.

We need to pay attention to the name of this fair: Vanity Fair. The most famous verse in the Bible that contains the word "vanity" is Ecclesiastes 1:2. The KJV Bible writes, "Vanity of vanities, vanity of vanities, all is vanity." In the NIV Bible, "vanity" is written as "meaningless."

In *The Pilgrim's Progress*, John Bunyan tells us that all the things that look splendid that are sold at Vanity Fair are actually of no value at all. However, people of this world struggle and stake their lives on these meaningless things, deceived into believing that they are of tremendous value.

The reason that these things are valueless is because they are apart from God and also draw us away from God. The entire message of Ecclesiastes points this out. It says that the pursuit of wisdom and knowledge apart from God is meaningless.

> "For with much wisdom comes much sorrow; the more knowledge, the more grief" (Eccles. 1:18).

It speaks of the vanity of knowledge. It says that pursuit of pleasure apart from God is also in vain(Eccles. 2:1-11).

> "I thought in my heart, 'Come now, I will test you with pleasure to find out what is good.' But that also proved to be meaningless" (Eccles. 2:1).

This is a testimony of someone who has staked his life on pleasure. Further, he says that the pursuit of material wealth is also meaningless.

> "All his days his work is pain and grief; even at night his mind does not rest. This too is meaningless"(Eccles. 2:23).

It testifies that the more wealth is stored up, the more pain it takes to manage it, and the easier it is to lose peace of heart. How true is this? The author of Ecclesiastes, King Solomon, was a king who enjoyed a great amount of knowledge, pleasure, and material wealth. He had 1,400 personal chariots, 12,000 guards, 700 queens, and 300 concubines - 1,000 women in total. Silver imported from Egypt was used as bricks for the palace and cedar wood as if it were mulberry wood.

However, what was the final confession of this man who enjoyed the greatest knowledge, greatest wealth, and greatest pleasures in this world? "Meaningless! Meaningless! Utterly meaningless! Everything is meaningless." The word *hebel* which is used in the verse to mean "in vain" originally indicated a breath blown in cold wintertime that fades quickly after forming an arc in the air. Like James' testimony, the reality of life in this world is "a mist that appears for a little while and then vanishes"(James 4:14).

Second, the true value we are to pursue in this world is the Truth.

What does "true value" mean? John Bunyan says that Truth is the true value. To the pilgrims who do not even give one look to the splendid things on display at the fair, a merchant asks, "What will you buy?" Christian and Faithful firmly reply, "We buy the truth."

This is quoted from Proverbs 23:23:

> "Buy the truth and do not sell it; get wisdom, discipline and understanding."

In the New Testament, Jesus teaches that He himself is the truth by saying: "I am the way and the truth and the life"(John 14:6).

> "Then you will know the truth, and the truth will set you free" (John 8:32).

However, truth is not an abstract or a metaphysical principle. In John 8:36, Jesus says, "So if the Son sets you free, you will be free indeed." Preceding this in verse 31, Jesus says, "If you hold to my teaching, you are really my disciples."

When we make Jesus Christ as Lord and abide in His Word, we live as truly free people who are set free from all vanity. However, because we are tempted by what we see, as we walk through Vanity Fair we need to hold onto the prayer that the pilgrims repeatedly prayed.

"Turn away mine eyes from beholding vanity."

To overcome all temptations, we need a spiritual hunger that overpowers the temptations. This desire must be towards the ultimate truth. It must be a desire not for the things of the world that disappear, but for the eternal things that cannot disappear.

> "The world and its desires pass away, but the man who does the will of God lives forever" (1 John 2:17).

Therefore, the writer of Ecclesiastes proclaims that the ultimate value of life is to "fear God." To be honest, if we stop before finishing the whole of Ecclesiastes, it is easy to fall into nihilism. To understand a book well, we need endurance to reach the conclusion, and it is especially the case with Ecclesiastes. I have often heard that there are people who fell into nihilism while reading Ecclesiastes and turned away from life.

What is the essence of Ecclesiastes? It is that knowledge, wealth, pleasure and fame are all in vain. Then what is the point of living? The conclusion lies here:

> "Now all has been heard; here is the conclusion of the matter: Fear God and keep his commandments, for this is the whole duty of man"(Eccles. 12:13).

It is only by fearing God, receiving His Son Jesus Christ as our Lord, and holding onto His Word and living it out that we are guaranteed a valuable life with no regrets.

Third, true value is always passed on.

In *The Pilgrim's Progress*, the pilgrims who pass through Vanity Fair become the subject of persecution and ridicule because they are so different from the people at the fair. First, their attire is different, which means that their lifestyle is different from others. Second, their manner of speech is different. There is a saying that goes, "Language as the house of being." Our speech reveals our souls. Third, they are ignorant to the things sold at Vanity Fair. Put more accurately, their interest in the Truth causes a relative ignorance to the things of the world.

For these reasons, the pilgrims are arrested, put on trial, and given the death sentence. It is persecution for righteousness. Faithful is taken first, scourged, lanced with knives, and burnt to ashes at the Stake. What sins have they committed to go through such suffering? This is exactly what life is. However, if the story were to end here, where would God's justice be?

There is one person who is moved by Faithful who does not deny his faith even in the midst of facing death. He sees in Faithful's last moment the reality of Truth that is stronger than the sword. His name is Hopeful. After escaping prison with God's protection, Christian re-embarks on his journey with Hopeful. Hopeful is the legacy of Faithful.

Truth does not die. Truth gives birth to truth, and disciples give birth to disciples. The righteous raise the righteous, and value gives birth to value. Value is passed down unchanged throughout history. Just as it is written in the Word, those who do God's will live forever. Therefore, we must not be discouraged when doing good. In due season, we will be reaping.

Let us look at verse 14, the last verse of Ecclesiastes.

> "For God will bring every deed into judgment, including every hidden thing, whether it is good or evil."

God is the final Judge of righteousness. Truth is passed on because the Judge is alive. In the world, we see unrighteousness temporarily defeating righteousness, and evil devouring good. Of course, the last judgment of humanity will make right all the irony in history. In this world, we will finally see truth marching on with the Almighty's intervention. We will see the ultimate value be passed down.

There is a story about Jim Elliot, a martyr of our generation. After graduating in the 1950s as the valedictorian from Wheaton College, a prestigious Christian university, he approached the Waodani tribe in Ecuador, Latin America with four of his friends. The tribe had never heard the gospel before. However, all of them lost their lives on that riverside at a young age. They all had guns for self-defense with them, but there was no trace of anyone having taken them out. They could not turn their guns toward those they were to love and evangelize to. Instead, they gave them their lives.

When the news spread, a reporter of Life magazine wrote of this incident, "What a waste." How did the wife of Jim Elliot reply to this?

She said, "No, it wasn't a waste."

Then she released in public a part of the journals that her husband Jim Elliot had written during college. There, the following prayer was written:

"Lord, make my way prosperous not that I achieve high station, but that my life be an exhibit to the value of knowing God."

It is followed by his well-known confession.

"He is no fool who gives up what he cannot keep to gain that which he cannot lose."

This is not the end of Jim Elliot's story. His wife went back to the village where her husband died, the village that killed her husband. The village people who saw Elizabeth Elliot threw their gates wide-open (this was possible because it was in the village's custom not to hurt women). The village was evangelized, and Truth had victory. The value of the Gospel finally became the new way of life for the villagers.

Please remember the lesson that our investment in true value inherits eternal value.

Questions for the Pilgrimage of Faith

1. What are the three lessons we can learn from Vanity Fair?

   1)

   2)

   3)

2. What differences did the pilgrims have from the people at Vanity Fair?

3. Who was the new companion of Christian after Faithful was martyred? What are his characteristics?

4. Share what we can learn from the martyr Jim Elliot.

When we make Jesus Christ as Lord and abide in His Word,
we live as truly free people, who are set free from all vanity.
To overcome all temptations, we need a spiritual hunger
that holds us stronger than the temptations.
This desire must be towards the ultimate truth.

2 Timothy 4:10

…for Demas, because he loved this world, has deserted me and has gone to Thessalonica. Crescens has gone to Galatia, and Titus to Dalmatia.

Genesis 19:26

But Lot's wife looked back, and she became a pillar of salt.

Pilgrim's Progress 21

Lesson of Demas

Red Light on the Pilgrimage

Among pilgrims on the journey of faith, there are some foolish and pitiable people who start well but suddenly return to their past because of one wrong choice. The typical example in the Bible is Demas. John Bunyan, the author of *The Pilgrim's Progress*, introduces Demas on the pilgrimage road to give an important warning to pilgrims.

Not long after they leave Vanity Fair, Christian and Hopeful meet a friend named "By-ends." While professing himself to be a pilgrim, By-ends is a man who lives like an opportunist, attentive only to secular interests.

Christian and Hopeful reject the temptation from "Mr. Hold-the-world," "Mr. Money-love" and "Mr. Save-all" who are with By-ends. They arrive at a silver mine, past an open field, and it is there they run into a decent-looking gentleman who is Demas. What would be the lesson that Demas gives to today's postmodern pilgrims?

Demas' Lesson to the Pilgrims

First, be on guard against love for the world.
Demas stops the pilgrims and tells them that there is something he wants to show them. He tempts them by saying, "Here is a silver mine, and some digging in it for treasure; if you will come, with a little pains you may richly provide for yourselves." He insists that they should come over to see the silver mine.

At this moment, Christian firmly says:

"Demas, thou art an enemy to the right ways of the Lord of this way, and hast been already condemned for thine own turning aside, by one of His Majesty's judges."

Christian is referring to the Bible here.

> "…for Demas, because he loved this world, has deserted me and has gone to Thessalonica" (2 Tim. 4:10).

By this verse alone, there is no way to know what is specifically meant by the phrase: "he loved this world." However, as the early church documents testify, we can understand that Demas turned away from the faith. In 1 John 2:15, we come across a warning: "Do not love the world." But the very next verse teaches the essence of what love for the world is.

> "For everything in the world—the lust of the flesh, the lust of the eyes, and the pride of life—comes not from the Father but from the world" (1 John 2:16).

Hence, the essence of love for the world here ultimately means the lust of the flesh, the lust of the eyes, and the pride of life. It seems that John Bunyan tried to illustrate Demas' love for the world with "the love for the silver mine" based on this passage. Obsession over silver and gold is the essence of love for the world.

Learning that following Jesus as a disciple does not guarantee material gain, Demas jumped into developing the silver mine.

If Demas was a true disciple of Jesus, he should have said something like the following: "Silver or gold I do not have, but I give you what I do have—the name of Jesus Christ of Nazareth" (refer to Acts 3:6). But unfortunately, Demas chose silver and gold, and he left to Thessalonica where the memories of silver and gold were sweet. It seems that Thessalonica was Demas' hometown. Demas was returning to the secular life to gain riches for himself. His time was not flowing to the future but back to the past.

Second, be on guard against self-assurance.

In *The Pilgrim's Progress*, Christian's companion Hopeful nearly falls for Demas' temptation. Then Christian shouts to Demas, asking:

"Is not the place dangerous? Hath it not hindered many in their pilgrimage?"

Demas answers:

"Not very dangerous, except to those that are careless."

In other words, Demas is saying that a little bit of desire is manageable if we are a little more careful. But is this true? Every temptation that leads to addiction starts from such confidence: "I can easily overcome this much desire!" But hear James' warning:

> "Then, after desire has conceived, it gives birth to sin; and sin, when it is full-grown, gives birth to death" (James 1:15).

The common characteristic of people with addictions is that they do not admit their addiction. Once they admit it, there is hope for healing. However, it is rarely the case that an addict acknowledges the severity of his addiction. Just like Demas, they say that it is "not very dangerous." Ask an alcoholic if he or she is an alcoholic. What would be the reply? It would be, "I'm just a little fond of drinking." Ask a gambling addict if he or she is addicted to gambling. The person would probably say, "I just enjoy it a little bit. It's like sports." What would a porn addict say if asked the same question? The person would say, "It's just that I enjoy a little bit of sexual fantasy for some mental relaxation."

But once they are addicted, they cannot come out of the mire. This is called a "withdrawal symptom." It is when someone has an obsession to the point where they feel that they may die if they do not satisfy their addiction. This is why they become slaves to alcohol, gambling, and porn their whole life.

It is the same with the desire for money or material wealth. We say, "It's just that I need money, and I like money a little bit." However, we need to remember that in a moment of carelessness, we can become slaves to materialism. No one should have confidence when it comes to desires. We must always be careful and always be on guard.

This is why the religious reformists referred to the fall of man as "total depravity" and the human existence as "total corruption." There is no part in our intelligence, sensibility, or will that is not depraved and corrupted. We must never overestimate our fallen selves. Being self-assured is not a desirable virtue for us to have on the journey of faith. We should not be full of self-assurance but full of God.

That's right. We are people who, without being filled with the Holy Spirit, can never be off guard even for a moment. We can never lead ourselves to holy ground without the help of God. With no such awareness, By-ends and his fellow men enter the silver mine as soon as they run into Demas. John Bunyan states that they were never seen again on the pilgrimage road. At this sight, Christian sings:

> "By-ends and silver Demas both agree;
> One calls; the other runs, that he may be
> A sharer in his lucre; so these two
> Take up in this world, and no farther go."

Third, remember Lot's wife.

Not long after they part with Demas, Christian and Hopeful discover an old monument. They find a strange inscription on the upper part of the monument. After struggling to interpret it, Christian finds out that it says, "Remember Lot's wife." It is another word of warning to the pilgrims who continue their pilgrimage journey. In fact, this is a recurring message from Demas' lesson. Originally, it comes from Genesis 19:26.

> "But Lot's wife looked back, and she became a pillar of salt."

Christian says to Hopeful as he interprets this message:

"Ah, my brother! this is a seasonable sight. It came just in time to us after the invitation which Demas gave us to come over to view the hill Lucre; and, had we gone over, as he desired us, and as thou wast inclining to do, my brother, we had, for aught I know, been made ourselves, like this woman, a spectacle for those that shall come after to behold."

Then Hopeful confesses as well:

"I am sorry that I was so foolish, and am made to wonder that I am not now as Lot's wife; for wherein was the difference betwixt her sin and mine? She only looked back, and I had a desire to go see. Let God's goodness be praised; and let me be ashamed that ever such a thing should be in mine heart."

We come to realize that there is something common among our spiritual forefathers who completed the race with no shame. It is a hunger, a holy desire for the crown as the prize. Remember what Apostle Paul says in 2 Timothy 4:7-8 before he expresses his regrets about Demas.

> "I have fought the good fight, I have finished the race, I have kept the faith. Now there is in store for me the crown of righteousness, which the Lord, the righteous Judge, will award to me on that day."

Our forefathers, all who believed in Jesus Christ, did not lose their salvation. But they feared one thing, which was receiving a shameful salvation. Our forefathers of faith often expressed this fear by saying that they were afraid that they would receive hats made out of dog fur while others would receive golden crowns.

Many years ago, I once visited Tunisia in Africa. The missionary who was showing us the area of Carthage, Tunisia's capital city in the past, told me to take a look at the sign on the narrow road. On it was written "Cyprian Road."

It was around 275 AD when Christians were being persecuted by Emperor Valerian Rome. Cyprian, the Bishop of Carthage during that time, reproached and encouraged the Christians who only sought worldly blessings and were not ready to be persecuted for righteousness. Cyprian was martyred in 278 AD as he was beheaded. One church historian testified to his life as the following: "Cyprian went the way that he had to go without any shame." For this reason, the road that Cyprian walked on still remains in Tunisia, where Islam is widespread today.

What kind of road do we need to walk on? Our choice between the shameless path of faith that Apostle Paul, Peter, and Cyprian took, or the way of Demas and Lot's wife, all hinges on our faith.

Questions for the Pilgrimage of Faith

1. What are the three lessons that Demas from *The Pilgrim's Progress* gives to today's pilgrims?
1)
2)
3)

2. Among the three lessons, what is the one that you need to be mindful of especially? Why?

3. What is an area that you are overconfident about, that you always need to be on guard against?

4. What is a common characteristic of our forefathers of faith who completed the race without shame? Answer after reflecting on the road we are to take.

We are people who, without being filled with the Holy Spirit,

can never be off guard even for a moment.

We can never lead ourselves to holy ground

without the help of God.

Acts 12:1-10

It was about this time that King Herod arrested some who belonged to the church, intending to persecute them. He had James, the brother of John, put to death with the sword. When he saw that this met with approval among the Jews, he proceeded to seize Peter also. This happened during the Festival of Unleavened Bread. After arresting him, he put him in prison, handing him over to be guarded by four squads of four soldiers each. Herod intended to bring him out for public trial after the Passover. So Peter was kept in prison, but the church was earnestly praying to God for him. The night before Herod was to bring him to trial, Peter was sleeping between two soldiers, bound with two chains, and sentries stood guard at the entrance. Suddenly an angel of the Lord appeared and a light shone in the cell. He struck Peter on the side and woke him up. "Quick, get up!" he said, and the chains fell off Peter's wrists. Then the angel said to him, "Put on your clothes and sandals." And Peter did so. "Wrap your cloak around you and follow me," the angel told him. Peter followed him out of the prison, but he had no idea that what the angel was doing was really happening; he thought he was seeing a vision. They passed the first and second guards and came to the iron gate leading to the city. It opened for them by itself, and they went through it. When they had walked the length of one street, suddenly the angel left him.

Pilgrim's Progress 22

Prison of Despair

When Captivated by Giant Despair

There is a Chinese idiom called "Si Mian Chu Ge." It is an expression used to illustrate a hopeless situation of being sieged by the enemy on all sides. The story takes place when Xiang Yu from the State of Chu and Liu Bang from the State of Han were in a battle against each other. Xiang Yu from Chu was in a plight as he was besieged by Han Xin, the great military general of Han. The food ran out, the soldiers became demoralized, and the enemy closed in.

Then in the middle of the night, the Chu's songs started to be heard on all sides. Han Xin of Han had forced the Chu captives to sing the songs of their nation. It was a mind game. As they heard songs from home, the already exhausted Chu soldiers became homesick, completely losing their spirits, and started abandoning their weapons. Eventually the soldiers renounced the battle, and the war came to an end as Xiang Yu committed suicide. Si Mian Chu Ge is an expression referring to this ancient event.

In *The Pilgrim's Progress*, a similar event happens to Christian. He falls into a pit not so much after he enters a comfortable-looking byway on the pilgrimage road. Coming out of the pit after a great struggle, Christian finds a shack where he falls asleep out of fatigue.

However, it is here where Christian becomes locked up in a dungeon called Doubting Castle as he is held captive by Giant Despair. Giant Despair has a wife named Distrust, who so urges Christian and Hopeful: "No one has ever made it out of this dungeon alive. Choose to make an end of yourselves rather than living with so much misery."

Christian comes to think that there is no other way but to follow her words. Yet, Hopeful proposes that they endure and wait, for they cannot go against the Lord's teachings by choosing to die according to her advice nor can they commit murder. Is not this situation fit for the expression Si Mian Chu Ge, or "the Prison of Despair"? We often come upon such situations on our life's pilgrimage.

It was the same for Apostle Peter. King Herod(Herod Agrippa the first, grandson of Herod the emperor) arrested Peter after killing James, the brother of John, who was a leader of the Jerusalem church. It would make sense that he who killed James would kill Peter who was a more influential leader than James. However, he had to postpone the trial and execution because it was during the Feast of Unleavened Bread. King Herod had Peter locked up in prison and ordered soldiers to strictly guard it.

Peter faced an inevitable death. What could he possibly do at that moment? Peter was literally in Si Mian Chu Ge, locked in the Prison of Despair. But God had mercy on him and miraculously freed him from the prison.

Here's a lesson we can learn from the pilgrims who end up in the Prison of Despair in life. What can we do in order to be freed from the Prison of Despair?

What We Can Do in the Prison of Despair

First, we need to trust God's Providence.

Acts 12:2 records, "He had James, the brother of John, put to death with the sword." John lived the longest among Jesus' 12 disciples, and James' life ended the earliest. John faced natural death, having lived a long life, and his brother James was martyred, executed by beheading. Though they were brothers, they lived completely different lives. We call this Providence. We see that God led the disciples in His providence with unique plans for their lives.

Likewise, after James was martyred, Peter was arrested once again. What would happen to Peter now? No one knew; only God did. But if we are people of God who believe in His sovereign providence, we also need to believe that His providence is good.

> "And we know that in all things God works for the good of those who love him, who have been called according to his purpose" (Rom. 8:28).

It seems that Peter trusted God's good providence. How else could he fall asleep while in chains? How could this be possible? It could have been either he gave up or believed in His providence. I believe that it was the latter case.

In *The Pilgrim's Progress*, the person who trusts God's providence more firmly in the Prison of Despair is not Christian but his companion Hopeful. He says that it is not up to Giant Despair to decide the outcome of the situation. He says that it is up to God and that they should wait and see, trusting His providence. He also says that an opportunity will surely come, and so they ought to have hope, refusing the temptation to take their own lives. John Bunyan writes that "With these words, Hopeful at present did calm the mind of his brother."

Yes, the more dire our situation is, the more patient we need to be in trusting God's good and sovereign providence. There is a verse that our spiritual forefathers held onto when placed in such desperate circumstances.

"…but the one who stands firm to the end will be saved"(Matt. 24:13).

If you are in the Prison of Despair, you need to trust in God's good providence.

Second, we need to pray earnestly.

There must have been a couple of actions that the early church could have taken when they found out that Peter was locked in the Prison of Despair: bribing King Herod since he liked money or recruiting an emergency rescue squad that would break into the prison and save Peter. But see what the early church chose to do:

> "So Peter was kept in prison, but the church was earnestly praying to God for him"(Acts 12:5).

The early church chose earnest prayer. Here the word "earnest" comes from *ektenes* in Greek, which corresponds with the word "intensely" or "fervently," meaning "to use up one's energy." It is not simply a prayer, but a petition. General situations require general prayers, but extraordinary situations require extraordinary prayers. The church's unified petition brought about the miracle that opened the door of the Prison of Despair.

Let us go back to *The Pilgrim's Progress*. In the prison, Christian and Hopeful, who even thought of committing suicide, realize that they had forgotten prayer. John Bunyan explains as follows.

> "…about midnight, they began to pray, and continued in prayer till almost break of day. Now, a little before it was day, good Christian thought of a solution."

Their prayer and petition allows them to find the solution to the problem. This is true. Anxiety, worry, and despair are not the solution. That is why a praise song we sing contains this confession:

> "Why worry when you can pray? / Why worry when you are praying? / Why the disappointment when you can pray? / Why wander around when you pray? / Kneel before God and pray. / Why worry when you can pray / purifying your heart and with all your heart? / Why worry when you are praying?"

Their prayer which starts on Saturday night continues until Sunday morning. And finally on the day of resurrection, they experience the miracle of resurrection. Do you need a resurrection? Pray. No, give petition. According to Acts 12:7, the moment they started praying "suddenly an angel of the Lord appeared and a light shone in the cell." This is the start of God's intervention and work through the angel. This is the outcome of petition. Are you in the Prison of Despair? Then now is the time to pray earnestly.

Third, we need to obey the Word.

The petition of the early church initiated the intervention of the angel of the LORD. Now the angel gave a message to rescue Peter.

In the latter half of verse 7, the angel says, "Quick, get up." In verse 8 he says, "Put on your clothes and sandals," and "wrap your cloak around you and follow me." All that Peter had to do was obey his words. "Peter followed him" (verse 9). And the result was breaking free from the prison, obtaining freedom.

> "They passed the first and second guards and came to the iron gate leading to the city. It opened for them by itself, and they went through it. When they had walked the length of one street, suddenly the angel left him" (Acts 12:10).

When we read the Bible or hear the experiences of the Lord's people, we can see that this is a very common way in which God works for His people who are in the Prison of Despair. God first leads us to fall on the cold floor of the prison and pray. He makes us give petition. And then He gives a Word of promise. The moment we hold on to the Word of promise and obey, the prison opens. The story of freedom begins.

In *The Pilgrim's Progress*, the moment he embraces the dawn of resurrection with earnest prayer, Christian shouts as if he had a sudden realization.

"What a fool am I to lie in a foul-smelling dungeon, when I may as well walk at liberty! I have a key in my bosom called Promise, that will, I am sure, open any lock in Doubting Castle."

Hopeful's face lights up. "That is good news, good brother: pluck it out of thy bosom, and try." Christian pulls the key out of his bosom and opens the door. As he turns the key, the bolt gives back, and the door flies open. Christian and Hopeful squeeze out all their strength to escape from Giant Despair's territory and return to the King's highway.

Long ago in the dying days of the Kingdom of Judea, there was a prophet locked in a prison. His name was Jeremiah, the weeping prophet. He shares the secret to escaping the Prison of Despair to us as the following.

> "Call to me and I will answer you and tell you great and unsearchable things you do not know"(Jer. 33:3).

But the answer that provided the secret to Jeremiah can be found in Jeremiah 33:1 that precedes verse 3.

> "While Jeremiah was still confined in the courtyard of the guard, the word of the Lord came to him a second time"(Jer. 33:1).

The prophet found the prescription for saving his people and himself through the Word of promise. Should we not also cry out in prayer as well? And should we not turn our ears to the Word of promise, the Word of hope? Would you not stand up, holding onto this hope?

A young man stayed up many nights drawing, hoping to become a painter. He took some of his paintings and wandered around an all-girls' middle school in Donam-dong, Marronnier Park, and a public library, but no one bought his paintings. He could not lift up his head. However, he did not fall into despair, even when he was exhausted from working in the factory in a uniform covered with oil stains or when he had to load numerous low-grade apples on a truck and hide from people to take a bite of one. How could he do that? Hear what he says.

"I was not in despair because of Dostoyevski and Hermann Hesse. I was not in despair because of God."

It took 7 years for him to prepare his book as a writer. He visited five different publishing companies but was rejected. But the sixth publisher decided to publish his book. And his second book was read by more than 3 million readers. This is the story of the best selling author Cheol Hwan Lee who wrote *Yeontangil* and *A Happy Junk Shop*. In *Yeontangil* there are 31 paintings that he drew night after night. The paintings that were rejected on the street are now revived in many readers' heart with a bright smile.

The first painting that Cheol Hwan Lee drew was a woodpecker. Drawing the woodpecker flapping in the sky, he was dreaming of his future and praying even in the midst of despair. That was the secret of how he opened the Prison of Despair.

Questions for the Pilgrimage of Faith

1. What are the things we need to do in order to break out of the Prison of Despair?

1)

2)

3)

2. What are the evil thoughts that Giant Despair's wife Mrs. Distrust suggests?

3. When Christian nearly falls into temptation, Hopeful raises him up. What is the message of Hopeful's encouragement?

4. Share about the prison that you are in today and what you have determined to do in order to escape from it.

The more dire our situation is, the more patient we need to be in trusting God's good and sovereign providence.

Ezekiel 34:12-16

As a shepherd looks after his scattered flock when he is with them, so will I look after my sheep. I will rescue them from all the places where they were scattered on a day of clouds and darkness. I will bring them out from the nations and gather them from the countries, and I will bring them into their own land. I will pasture them on the mountains of Israel, in the ravines and in all the settlements in the land. I will tend them in a good pasture, and the mountain heights of Israel will be their grazing land. There they will lie down in good grazing land, and there they will feed in a rich pasture on the mountains of Israel. I myself will tend my sheep and have them lie down, declares the Sovereign Lord. I will search for the lost and bring back the strays. I will bind up the injured and strengthen the weak, but the sleek and the strong I will destroy. I will shepherd the flock with justice.

Pilgrim's Progress 23

Delectable Mountains

Expectations for the True Shepherd

The sheep appears as the most general metaphor for human existence in the Bible.

> "We all, like sheep" (Isa. 53:6).

The Bible compares political or religious leaders who lead the sheep to "shepherds." Human history can be described as the repetitive cycle of expectations and disappointments in leadership. Every time the government changes, we carry hope for the new leadership with anticipation and thrill. However, such anticipation soon ends with great disappointment, and we wait for new leadership again.

The Bible calls such anticipation as "an anticipation for the true shepherd" by comparing it to the experience of false shepherds. In Ezekiel 34 appear two very contrasting verses. These verses show a clear contrast between false shepherds and the true shepherd.

> "You have not strengthened the weak or healed the sick or bound up the injured. You have not brought back the strays or searched for the lost. You have ruled them harshly and brutally" (Ezek. 34:4).

This is the portrayal of false shepherds.

> "I will search for the lost and bring back the strays. I will bind up the injured and strengthen the weak, but the sleek and the strong I will destroy. I will shepherd the flock with justice" (Ezek. 34:16).

In verse 16 we see the depiction of the true shepherd. In *The Pilgrim's Progress*, Christian suffers greatly because of the false shepherds he meets on his pilgrimage journey. Worldly-Wiseman, Talkative, By-ends, and Demas all represent false shepherds. Because of them, Christian is delayed and imprisoned. If only sufferings like these were to continue, our life's pilgrimage would be impossible.

But in *The Pilgrim's Progress*, although Christian experiences numerous obstacles and suffering, he is also strengthened with pleasant experiences at House Beautiful and at the Delectable Mountains. At the Delectable Mountains, Christian and Hopeful encounter good shepherds for the first time in a long time and hear helpful advice. Then what would be the lesson we learn about the shepherd we encounter at the Delectable Mountains?

Lessons about the Shepherd

First, we need to trust that our Lord is the Good Shepherd.
It is certainly a blessing to be under good political leaders as we live a life of pilgrims on this earth. An even greater blessing is to encounter good spiritual leaders in our lives. Pray that our children would meet good teachers and good pastors at school and at church as they grow up.

But there is one thing we should know. No respectable leader is perfect. Thus the Bible says that God ultimately sent his son Jesus Christ as the true and Good Shepherd of mankind. This is the gospel.

> "I am the good shepherd. The good shepherd lays down his life for the sheep" (John 10:11).

God who is the Father of Jesus already declared that He is the Good Shepherd in the Old Testament.

> "I myself will tend my sheep and have them lie down, declares the Sovereign Lord" (Ezek. 34:15).

Why is the shepherd important? We can grasp this more clearly when we understand the characteristics of sheep. I was born at a ranch in Omokchon near the outskirts of Suwon. This ranch, which has become today's Hwaseong Livestock Research Institute, reared cows and horses for the most part but sometimes raised sheep as well. So from a young age, I was able to closely observe sheep.

The characteristics of sheep that I experienced coincide exactly with those of people. Sheep look clean, but they easily get dirty.

This is why the Bible says that we are all like sheep. Sheep do not have a sense of direction. Most animals can find their way back home, but sheep cannot. More than anything sheep do not have any means to protect themselves. They have a lot of fear because they are vulnerable to attacks from outside.

All of the sheep's weaknesses can be resolved at once. They just need to meet a good shepherd. The shepherd washes them. The shepherd gives them direction. The shepherd protects them with a rod and a staff. The Bible declares that God, and His son Jesus Christ, is our Good Shepherd. Therefore it is a great privilege to encounter and believe in God, and His son Jesus, as our shepherd. This is the gospel we have experienced.

Second, we need to rejoice in the blessings of the shepherds.

Believing in the existence of the invisible God is still a difficult spiritual task for people. Therefore, God raises up shepherds, though imperfect, among those who trust and follow Him. The calling of mature shepherds is to lead believers who are like sheep to the way of salvation, to help them belong to a beautiful community where they can enjoy the blessings of spiritual protection and food.

Ezekiel 34:12 narrates God's calling as a shepherd. He says that

He will search for His sheep and rescue them. In verse 16 He declares that He will search for the lost and bring back those that are chased away. Christian doctrine(theology) defines this as the "call of salvation."

What I fear the most in ministry is that there might be people who attend church but depart from this world without the assurance of salvation. According to the parable of the Good Shepherd in Luke chapter 15, Jesus is the one who goes after the one lost sheep even if it means that he has to leave the 99 behind.

> "And when he finds it, he joyfully puts it on his shoulders"(Luke 15:5).

Jesus also holds a feast after returning with the lost sheep. There is a painting that I hung on a wall at home to always look at. It portrays Jesus our Shepherd with a sheep on his shoulders. "I can never lose this sheep." This is the heart of a shepherd.

A saying often used in the western world goes, "Count the sheep." This saying comes from the Bible. Shepherds could sleep well only after counting the sheep to make sure that all were present. "Sleep" in English resembles the word "sheep." Sometimes the correlation between the two words is explained by the fact that "sheep" sounds like "sleep" when it is repeated. Shepherds are those who can go to sleep only after finding all their sheep.

However, the call of a shepherd does not end with the salvation of souls. A shepherd needs to tend the saved sheep in good pastures. He needs to help the sheep enjoy the blessing of dwelling in his presence. There is only one reason why shepherds teach the Word, teach prayer, and encourage them to stay in the presence of the Holy Spirit. It is because they want to see the sheep experience joy in the Delectable Mountains. This is the experience of the Delectable Mountains. *The Pilgrim's Progress* depicts this scene as follows:

> "They went then till they came to the Delectable Mountains, which mountains belong to the Lord of that hill of which we have spoken before. So they went up to the mountains to behold the gardens and orchards, the vineyards and fountains of water, where also they drank and washed themselves, and did freely eat of the vineyards. Now there were on the tops of these mountains shepherds feeding their flocks, and they stood by the highway-side."

Let's look at the prophet Ezekiel's testimony.

> "I will tend them in a good pasture, and the fountain heights of Israel will be their grazing land. There they will lie down in good grazing land and there they will feed in a rich pasture on the mountains of Israel" (Ezek. 34:14).

This passage is a prophecy of blessing that the scattered Israelites would enjoy upon returning to the Promised Land and ultimately a promise of abundant life that Christians can enjoy through a church community. If the shepherds in your life that the Lord has raised are providing such blessings, enjoy the blessing. And appreciate the shepherds who share the blessed pasture with you.

Today, there definitely are false shepherds who elude the world and deceive people. Look out for them. But there still are good shepherds that God raises up and uses in this world. Praise the Lord for them. And enjoy the blessings shared through them and the joy of faith. Rejoice in the fact that our pilgrimage steps lead to the Delectable Mountains.

Third, we need to accept our shepherds' warning and be watchful.

The Pilgrim's Progress introduces the names of the shepherds that the pilgrims encounter at the Delectable Mountains. They are

Knowledge, Experience, Watchful, and Sincere. These show various spiritual roles of shepherds. Some shepherds show knowledge, some spiritual experience, some watchfulness, and others the example of a sincere life.

But what we need to focus on here is that shepherds are not those who only say things that are sweet to hear. A key role of a good shepherd is being watchful. Our pilgrimage has not ended yet, and we need to be alert in order to finish the race.

Therefore, if a shepherd's message only includes sweet words and no discipline, we need to doubt if he is a truthful shepherd. It is just as how parents who do not rebuke their children at all are questioned if they really are parents. The writer of Hebrews asks, "for what children are not disciplined by their father?"(Heb. 12:7). In that sense, he teaches us to better respect and trust leaders who reproach us spiritually.

> "Have confidence in your leaders and submit to their authority, because they keep watch over you as those who must give an account. Do this so that their work will be a joy, not a burden, for that would be of no benefit to you"(Heb. 12:7).

Now let's visit the scenes in which shepherds are showing different sites to the pilgrims at the Delectable Mountains. What is happening?

The shepherds lead the pilgrims to the mountaintop called Error. There is always a possibility of error on the pilgrimage of faith. Then the shepherds lead the pilgrims to another mountaintop called Caution. They warn the pilgrims that if they do not take caution, they could be casted into the Doubting Castle again. Afterwards they take the pilgrims to a valley with a rumbling fire. There is a by-way to Hell in the valley.

The last place the shepherds lead the pilgrims to at the very end is called Clear. There the pilgrims get a glimpse of the glory of the New Jerusalem through a telescope. That's right. We need to continue our journey of pilgrimage with our eyes fixed on the final glory of God's Kingdom shown through the shepherds' telescope. The pilgrims in *The Pilgrim's Progress* sing as follows as they depart from the Delectable Mountains:

> "Thus by the shepherds secrets are revealed,
> Which from all other men are kept concealed.
> Come to the shepherds, then, if you would see
> Things deep, things hid, and that mysterious be."

Now pilgrims, as you enjoy the blessings of your shepherds, shouldn't you also take their warning to be watchful and walk the remaining pilgrimage road with more caution? I pray that we would enjoy the glory of completion at the end of our pilgrimage journey.

Questions for the Pilgrimage of Faith

1. What are the three lessons about shepherds that we learn at the Delectable Mountains?
1)
2)
3)

2. The Bible says we are all like sheep. Share the common features that we share with sheep.

3. Talk about the scenes that the shepherds show the pilgrims at the Delectable Mountains in order. Share about the last scene especially.

4. Share about the help of the shepherds you met in your life's pilgrimage.

There is only one reason why shepherds teach the Word,

teach prayer, and encourage them to stay

in the presence of the Holy Spirit.

It is because they want to see the sheep experience joy

in the Delectable Mountains.

Galatians 2:11-16

When Cephas came to Antioch, I opposed him to his face, because he stood condemned. For before certain men came from James, he used to eat with the Gentiles. But when they arrived, he began to draw back and separate himself from the Gentiles because he was afraid of those who belonged to the circumcision group. The other Jews joined him in his hypocrisy, so that by their hypocrisy even Barnabas was led astray. When I saw that they were not acting in line with the truth of the gospel, I said to Cephas in front of them all, "You are a Jew, yet you live like a Gentile and not like a Jew. How is it, then, that you force Gentiles to follow Jewish customs? "We who are Jews by birth and not sinful Gentiles know that a person is not justified by the works of the law, but by faith in Jesus Christ. So we, too, have put our faith in Christ Jesus that we may be justified by faith in Christ and not by the works of the law, because by the works of the law no one will be justified.

Galatians 3:1-3

You foolish Galatians! Who has bewitched you? Before your very eyes Jesus Christ was clearly portrayed as crucified. I would like to learn just one thing from you: Did you receive the Spirit by the works of the law, or by believing what you heard? Are you so foolish? After beginning by means of the Spirit, are you now trying to finish by means of the flesh?

Pilgrim's Progress 24

Ignorance and Little Faith

For a Pleasant Pilgrimage of Faith

Whenever we travel long distances alone by airplane or train, we hope that someone pleasant would come sit next to us. For example, when a beautiful woman or handsome man approaches us, we often recite a prayer without even noticing. "Lord, Your will be done." However, when we see a rough-looking person who seems to have the possibility of ruining our mood, we have the tendency to pray, "Lord, lead us not into temptation."

This applies similarly to our church lives. We often come across people who have a tendency to stumble us. If we want a pleasant church life and pilgrimage of faith, we need to discern who they are and overcome the tests that they throw at us. If there are two categories of people who distract our journey of faith, the first would be those who believe incorrectly, and second, those who believe inconsistently. John Bunyan, the author of *The Pilgrim's Progress*, calls them Ignorance and Little-faith.

As Christian and Hopeful leave the Delectable Mountains and are passing through the village of Conceit, they run into a fellow named Ignorance. He is someone who boldly believes that as long as you live a righteous life in accordance with the laws, you can enter New Jerusalem. We could call him a moralist or legalist. However, he has never passed through the narrow gate.

The next pilgrim they meet is a man who met a robber on his journey and is limping from injury. He used to be a kind man and lived in a village called "Sincere." Unfortunately, he got lost one day and fell asleep, meeting three robbers who threatened him and stole his money. However, even in the midst of this he did not lose his treasure and the certificate to heaven. His name was "Little-faith."

He did not lose his faith completely, but because of his little faith, he was in terrible spiritual condition. Whenever we meet such people within the church, we experience spiritual tests and confusion.

During the time of the early church, the church of Galatia experienced such trials and confusion because of these people. At that time, there were many legalists within the church. They had fundamentally wrong beliefs and confused those who rightly believed in the gospel. Apostle Paul, just like John Bunyan, called them "foolish."

> "You foolish Galatians! Who has bewitched you? Before your very eyes Jesus Christ was clearly portrayed as crucified" (Gal. 3:1).

In Galatians chapter 2, Paul reproves believers of little faith or those who have lost consistency. He mentions Peter, whom Paul could not help but rebuke, as a representative of such people. Likewise, let us first think about those of the first category: those who often appear in our churches and throw us into confusion, those who have little faith.

Two Types of People
Who Become Obstacles in Our Journey of Faith

First, we must beware of Little-faith who has lost consistency.

The greatest reason that "Little-faith" succumbed to the robbers was fear. Because of fear, Little-faith was confounded and was unable to act with consistency. We see this in Peter. In Galatians 2:11, we see Cephas, Peter, being reproved by Paul in Antioch.

> "For before certain men came from James, he used to eat with the Gentiles. But when they arrived, he began to draw back and separate himself from the Gentiles because he was afraid of those who belonged to the circumcision group" (Gal. 2:12).

At that time, James was the leader of the Jerusalem church. It seems that one day a group of Jewish Christians arrived at the gentile city of Antioch. Until then, Peter, who had devoted himself to the evangelical work for gentiles, believed that gentiles were not unclean and that they were not subjects to be avoided. He ate with them and served them. However, as the Jewish Christians who believed that Jews and Gentiles should not mix arrived, Peter changed his attitude and acted as though he did not want to eat with the gentiles.

This verse states that Peter did not eat with them because he was afraid. Perhaps he was overcome with the fear of being cast out by the Jewish leaders. How disappointed would the gentile believers of Antioch be, seeing his inconsistent behavior?

In fact, losing consistency and being ruled by fear was Peter's lifelong weakness, like an Achilles' tendon. And at this point, he had still not overcome his weakness. This was the same reason that Peter denied Jesus. He was fearful of the disadvantages and suffering that he might face when it was revealed that he was His disciple.

Let's go a little further back in time. Peter is walking on the roaring waters of the Sea of Galilee. The reason that he is able to walk on water for even just a little while was that he believed the word of Jesus: "Come." Yet a while later, Peter sees the wind that was blowing over the sea water, becomes afraid, and sinks into the water, shouting "Jesus, save me." Try to recall Jesus's words at this moment.

> "Immediately Jesus reached out his hand and caught him. 'You of little faith,' he said, 'why did you doubt?'" (Matt. 14:31).

Here we can see again Peter being inconsistent and overwhelmed by fear. Do not forget that Jesus called him "you of little faith." Peter was not one who had no faith. If he did not have faith, he would not have even stepped out of the boat. However, he lacked consistent faith, faith that continually depends on Jesus.

Jesus calls the following those of "little faith": those who show different faces at the church, home or workplace, those who have double-sided faith, having different faces when they are strong and when they are in trials. John Bunyan the author of *The Pilgrim's Progress* gets an idea here and introduces a character called Little-faith.

In fact, John Bunyan states through the words of Little-faith that if we do not want to be overcome with fear and leave Jesus' side as Peter did, we must arm ourselves with the shield of faith. We must continuously pray for Jesus' protection as we walk our pilgrimage road. Now, let us listen to the song of Christian.

> "Poor Little-Faith! Have you been among the thieves?
> Were you robbed? Remember this, whosoever believes
> And gets more faith shall then a victor be
> Over ten thousand, else scarce over three."

Second, we must beware of Ignorance who has the wrong belief.

In *The Pilgrim's Progress*, when Ignorance meets Christian for the first time he asks, "Where are you going?" Of course, Christian replies that he is going to the New Jerusalem. When Christian asks Ignorance what he will say in order to open the gates of New Jerusalem, Ignorance without an ounce of hesitation replies as the following:

"I know my Lord's will, and have been a good liver; I pay every man his own; I pray, fast, pay money to the church and give to the poor."

Everything that Ignorance mentions is necessary. However, the problem is whether or not they are the requirements of salvation that the Bible teaches us. The biggest reason that this young man is named "Ignorance" is that he is ignorant of the biblical way of salvation. Let us again listen to the way of salvation as declared by Paul.

> "…know that a person is not justified by the works of the law, but by faith in Jesus Christ. So we, too, have put our faith in Christ Jesus that we may be justified by faith in Christ and not by the works of the law, because by the works of the law no one will be

justified"(Gal. 2:12).

Many who attended the church of Galatia had the same beliefs as those of Ignorance from *The Pilgrim's Progress*. This was a result of those who were unable to abandon the so-called Jewish traditions, the influence of the Judaists and the legalists. The apostle Paul points to those in the church of Galatia who are wavering in their faith by this influence and calls them foolish and spiritually ignorant people.

> "You foolish Galatians! Who has bewitched you? Before your very eyes Jesus Christ was clearly portrayed as crucified"(Gal. 3:1).

Why does the apostle Paul talk about the cross here? If we can be forgiven of our sins and be justified as righteous by keeping the law and having good morals, why did Jesus come and carry the cross?

> "I do not set aside the grace of God, for if righteousness could be gained through the law, Christ died for nothing!"(Gal. 2:21).

Christian and Hopeful meet Ignorance once more. At this time

Ignorance answers that he needs to believe in Christ in order to be called righteous. He says that he believes in God and in heaven. However, as they enter into a deeper conversation Ignorance states that no matter how much he believes in Christ, he believes that on top of Christ's work, he will be called righteous based on his efforts in fulfilling the duties of faith. Eventually, Ignorance is saying that his ultimate righteousness is founded upon his efforts and deeds.

At last Ignorance shouts, "Would you have us trust in what Christ alone has accomplished without adding our own accomplishments?" This is the reality of Ignorance's faith. After all, his belief is based on the equation: Faith + Deed = Salvation. This was the nature of the legalists within the church of Galatia. What does the Apostle Paul tell them?

> "Are you so foolish? After beginning by means of the Spirit, are you now trying to finish by means of the flesh?" (Gal. 3:3).

If the basis of salvation is one's own efforts, then the basis of salvation is derived from the flesh. The religious reformers declared, "Sola Gratia" and "Sola Fide" to the church during the Middle Ages which suppressed and diluted people's faith by imposing many religious regulations other than faith in Christ's work on the cross. Today is also a time when "grace alone" and "faith alone" is urgently needed.

> "For it is by grace you have been saved, through faith—and this is not from yourselves, it is the gift of God— not by works, so that no one can boast"(Eph. 2:8-9).

This verse expressed in an algebra equation would be: "Grace + Faith – Deeds = Salvation." But then some misunderstand and ask, "Then does it mean that we have the freedom to live however we please?" This is never the case. One must solve this equation in the right way. Anyone who knows how to solve an algebra equation can solve it. One simply needs to move "deeds" to the other side. Then it becomes: Grace + Faith = Salvation + Deeds. Deeds should always follow those who have been saved. We cannot live our lives however we want. And yet, our actions cannot become a condition for our salvation. This is not because actions are unnecessary but because no one on earth can earn salvation through their own efforts. This is the heart of the Christian view of salvation. Being unaware of this truth is the essence and reality of Ignorance.

Before we finish reading *The Pilgrim's Progress*, we will run into Ignorance once more. Fortunately, he crosses the River of Death on his boat and arrives at the gate of the New Jerusalem. However, the problem is that the gates of Heaven do not open for him. As he knocks on the gates with all his might, some people appear above the gate and tell him that the gates open only to those who have their certificate.

The certificate proclaims Jesus as the only Savior and Lord. Ignorance does not have this certificate. Immediately, a group of shining angels appear before him, lift him up in an instance, and throw him into a dark tunnel before the gate. The tunnel leads directly to hell.

Have we prepared this certificate of faith? Or are we still walking the path of Ignorance according to our hearts and fleshly thoughts? Until what point will we continue to walk this path that deceives ourselves and leads others into confusion? Despite your belief in Christ, will you live your life inconsistently and double-mindedly, walking in little faith? Is your name Ignorance, Little-faith, or are you Christian the true pilgrim?

Questions for the Pilgrimage of Faith

1. Who are the two types of people who tempt Christian on his walk of faith?

1)

2)

2. Talk about the two types of people you have met in your walk of faith.

3. Share your thoughts on the Equation of Salvation.

4. Explain your answer to the last question: Is your name Ignorance, Little-faith, or are you Christian?

Our actions cannot become a condition for our salvation.
This is not because actions are unnecessary
but because no one on earth can earn salvation
through their own efforts.
This is the heart of the Christian view of salvation.

1 Thessalonians 5:1-11

Now, brothers and sisters, about times and dates we do not need to write to you, for you know very well that the day of the Lord will come like a thief in the night. While people are saying, "Peace and safety," destruction will come on them suddenly, as labor pains on a pregnant woman, and they will not escape. But you, brothers and sisters, are not in darkness so that this day should surprise you like a thief. You are all children of the light and children of the day. We do not belong to the night or to the darkness. So then, let us not be like others, who are asleep, but let us be awake and sober. For those who sleep, sleep at night, and those who get drunk, get drunk at night. But since we belong to the day, let us be sober, putting on faith and love as a breastplate, and the hope of salvation as a helmet. For God did not appoint us to suffer wrath but to receive salvation through our Lord Jesus Christ. He died for us so that, whether we are awake or asleep, we may live together with him. Therefore encourage one another and build each other up, just as in fact you are doing.

Pilgrim's Progress 25

Enchanted Ground

A Season of Spiritual Drought

In *The Pilgrim's Progress*, when Christian arrives at the Enchanted Ground, he is immediately lured into a deep sleep by the strange air that fills the place. As soon as he enters the village, Hopeful who feels the stiffening of his body and the drowsiness says to Christian, "I do now begin to grow so drowsy, that I can scarcely hold up mine eyes; let us lie down here, and take one nap."

Then Christian tells Hopeful that this is the place that one of the shepherds at the Delectable Mountains warned them of and that if they were to fall asleep here, they would never be able to wake up again.

Here we can learn that on our own pilgrimage journey, we will inevitably pass through the Enchanted Ground. Even one who has faithfully walked in faith will be tempted all of a sudden to go into a spiritual sleep. Although we might look very peaceful on the outside, we go through a period in which we cannot pray, lose interest in the Word, and experience the joy of praise dry up. Our forefathers of faith called this period a "spiritual dry season."

The church of Thessalonica experienced this dry season. The church of Thessalonica was born as a result of three weeks of preaching the gospel in the synagogue during Apostle Paul's second missionary journey(A.D. 50-53). In the early stages, the Thessalonian believers were overly hopeful about the Lord's return. They experienced a powerful revival of the Gospel, and stories of their faith spread far and wide.

However, they had one problem. They did not know how to prepare for Christ's coming. Some of them even gave up their daily duties in order to wait for Christ's return. But as the time of Christ's coming was delayed, they started to loosen up and fall into spiritual negligence and sleep. The book of Thessalonians is

Apostle Paul's letter addressed to warn them against spiritual sleep. Then what are the things that we need to do to be careful not to fall into spiritual sleep?

How to Guard Against Spiritual Sleep

First, we need to be alert especially during times of peace.

> "While people are saying, 'Peace and safety,' destruction will come on them suddenly, as labor pains on a pregnant woman, and they will not escape"(1 Thess. 5:3).

In times of peace and safety, we must be more alert. This is a critical time when it is easy to fall into spiritual sleep, just as it is dangerous for Christian and Hopeful when they arrive at the peaceful-looking Enchanted Ground past the Delectable Mountains.

> "So then, let us not be like others, who are asleep, but let us be awake and sober"(1 Thess. 5:6).

Spiritual relaxation comes not during a time of suffering or persecution, but during times of peace and safety. Satan tried to shake up the early church through persecution and caused great suffering as well as martyrdom. However, the early church rather stayed awake and prayed, which led to the beginning of revival in the early church.

> "And Saul approved of their killing him. On that day a great persecution broke out against the church in Jerusalem, and all except the apostles were scattered throughout Judea and Samaria" (Acts 8:1).

What was the consequence of this great persecution?

> "Those who had been scattered preached the word wherever they went. Philip went down to a city in Samaria and proclaimed the Messiah there" (Acts 8:4-5).

And in the following it is written, "So there was great joy in that city" (Acts 8:8). Persecution in Jerusalem led to the fruit of spiritual revival in Samaria.

If we look in the Bible, we can consistently observe how true crises in life come not during times of suffering but in times of peace after a victory. When we read through Joshua in the Old Testament, we see the Israelites after they defeat Jericho. They share the spoils with one another and have a festival of peace. Relaxed from the festivities, Joshua makes the poor decision of sending only two to three thousand soldiers to Ai, their next battle target. He refuses to send the full force of the troops. However, Joshua unexpectedly experiences great defeat and finally spends time in repentance and contrition.

This was also the case with David, a man after God's heart. When did the greatest trial of his life come? 2 Samuel 11:1 shows us that a war occurred while David was in the prime of his life, but he did not feel the need to go into the battle himself and sent only soldiers under him. The Bible states: "David remained in Jerusalem." And the next verse begins as follows: "One evening David got up from his bed" (2 Sam. 11:2).

Does this not show a side of a peaceful time in the prime of David's life when he did not even need to focus on his duties as a king? After having restful sleep, the king gets up in the evening, and during a walk on his balcony under the sunset, he sees a woman bathing, Bathsheba. From there begins David's downfall.

Therefore, we must be careful during times of peace and safety. Laying our guards down always brings about a tragedy.

Second, the most important thing is to live with God.

In times of peace, what is something that we constantly need to be careful to do? We can find the answer in 1 Thessalonians 5:10.

> "He died for us so that, whether we are awake or asleep, we may live together with him."

The most important thing is to be with God wherever and whenever. If Jesus is the true savior of our souls, it is our utmost priority to seek His presence and to search His will.

Do you know that it is possible for the Lord's disciples to do His work without ever consulting Him while doing whatever they please? Then what is the most important thing? It is to be with the Lord. Being spiritually armed is necessary for us to keep this priority.

> "But since we belong to the day, let us be sober, putting on faith and love as a breastplate, and the hope of salvation as a helmet"
> (1 Thess. 5:8).

Paul calls us to be on guard spiritually so that we might not repeat the tragedy of spiritual disarmament.

In the 1920s, there was a man named Frank Laubach who graduated from Princeton, Union, and Columbia University and went to the Philippines as an education missionary. Unfortunately, his ministry did not bear much fruit, and he even lost his health. One day as he went up a hill behind his house to pray, he was brought to tears realizing that having lost God's presence, he had grown weary of doing things according to his wisdom and understanding. The next moment, he realized that he was still praying while he was coming down the hill. Returning home, he decided to experiment with a prayer he called "Game with Minutes." He wanted to practice a spiritual exercise of thinking about God every moment he was awake. He recorded the following:

> "Can I bring God back in my mind-flow every few seconds so that God shall always be in my mind as an after image, shall always be one of the elements in every concept and precept? I choose to make the rest of my life as an experiment in answering this question."

An important lesson he learned from that day was the experience of work and prayer becoming one. Especially while he was working, he experienced a great transformation in his heart as he not only prayed for himself but also interceded for other people with flash prayers. On April 27th, 1937, he recorded what he felt

God was speaking to Him as the following:

> "My child, when you pray to Me of your own little troubles and doubts, your prayer is pretty thin and small. When you reach out to help other people by offering yourself as a channel for Me, your prayer becomes at once large and noble."

He confessed that since then, living each moment with God became more possible. And that's right. The most important thing is to live with God.

Third, we must live lives that encourage one another.
The last secret to being watchful of spiritual sleep is to live a life that encourages others.

> "Therefore encourage one another and build each other up, just as in fact you are doing"(1 Thess. 5:11).

In our life's pilgrimage road, when we become lazy and are about to fall into a spiritual sleep as though enchanted by magic, what is most important is our companions who wake us up and encourage us. In *The Pilgrim's Progress*, when Christian wakes up Hopeful and encourages him to be on guard, Hopeful thanks him as he is reminded of the the words from Ecclesiastes:

> "Two are better than one, because they have a good return for their labor: If either of them falls down, one can help the other up. But pity anyone who falls and has no one to help them up" (Eccles. 4:9-10).

Hope tells Christian, "Hitherto hath thy company been my help; and thou shalt have a good reward for thy labor." From there they continue their conversation in spiritual fellowship. To the church of Thessalonica which was on the verge of falling into a spiritual sleep, Paul continually emphasized this significant secret in his letter: "Love one another" (1 Thess. 4:9); "Encourage one another" (1 Thess. 4:18); "Encourage one another and build each other up" (1 Thess. 5:11).

Living in the 21st century, everyone wants to monopolize their life rather than share it. This is because we are forgetting that we all need one another. One theologian said that in order for believers' true fellowship to be restored within today's church, we must see one another as an adopted family member with a warm and open heart. One reason that adoptions often do not end happily is that people unnecessarily hide the truth about the adoption.

A mother wrote the following letter when her adopted child became old enough to understand words:

"My son, in this life, you will remember two special women. You may not remember the face of the first woman. The other woman you now call your mother. However, the truth is that both are your mothers.

One mother gave you life, the other gave you a family. One gave you the vast world, the other gave you a family, father, mother and siblings whom you could live this life with in that vast world. One mother gave you a nationality, the other gave you a name. One held your fragile little hands, the other will guide you to many other hands to hold throughout this life. One gave you talents, the other will guide you to set goals. One mother gave you emotions, the other will give you love and discipline for those emotions.

Lastly son, your first mother gave you this world, but the other mother, that is I, desires to help you live as a light in this world, to grow up as a blessed being."

Here, we are able to see the true reflection of the church as the spiritual family. I pray that our fellowship will share growth and blessings with one another.

Questions for the Pilgrimage of Faith

1. What can we do to be on guard against falling into a spiritual sleep?

1)

2)

3)

2. Think about your spiritual crisis and make a decision to overcome it.

3. Do you have a spiritual partner who will wake you and encourage you when you fall into a spiritual sleep? What help can you give to your fellow believers?

4. The most important thing is to be with God wherever and whenever. What is your priority?

Isaiah 62:1-5

For Zion's sake I will not keep silent, for Jerusalem's sake I will not remain quiet, till her vindication shines out like the dawn, her salvation like a blazing torch. The nations will see your vindication, and all kings your glory; you will be called by a new name that the mouth of the LORD will bestow. You will be a crown of splendor in the LORD's hand, a royal diadem in the hand of your God. No longer will they call you Deserted, or name your land Desolate. But you will be called Hephzibah, and your land Beulah; for the LORD will take delight in you, and your land will be married. As a young man marries a young woman, so will your Builder marry you; as a bridegroom rejoices over his bride, so will your God rejoice over you.

Pilgrim's Progress 26

The Land of Beulah

God's Promise that He Will End Our Sufferings

There exists a theological term called "theodicy." The word "theodicy" derives from the combination of two Greek words *theos*(God) and *dike*(justice). In the world we live in, there is suffering, hardship, pain, and evil that is hard to understand. Theodicy refers to the theological debate that discusses the following problem: "If the Christian God is all-powerful and good, how is He just when He allows pain and evil?"

The Bible refers to God's people as the chosen people. However, there are times when we must live as though we are abandoned, and there are moments when we need to pass through the desert rather than the promised land. In those times, we inevitably ask ourselves, "Does God really exist?" This is the question that theodicy deals with.

Yet, in Isaiah, God says that He knows that His people are going through such troubles, and He promises that He will end the time of pain and suffering.

> "No longer will they call you Deserted, or name your land Desolate. But you will be called Hephzibah, and your land Beulah; for the Lord will take delight in you, and your land will be married" (Isa. 62:4).

This verse means: "Even in the lives of the elect, there is suffering. But that is not the end. You will now be called Hephzibah and the land you are standing on will no longer be a desolate land, but a land where the new life of Beulah(married, bride) begins."

In *The Pilgrim's Progress*, there is countless suffering during Christian's pilgrimage despite the fact that he is traveling towards the New Jerusalem. He has to pass through the Hill of Suffering, the

Valley of Humility, the Valley of the Shadow of Death, and the Prison of Despair.

However, if the pilgrimage was filled only with suffering, pilgrims called by the Lord and chosen saints will find it difficult to endure. Fortunately, there are House Beautiful and the Delectable Mountains along the way. And finally, before crossing the River of Death, another place of encouragement called the Land of Beulah awaits Christian. What is the reason that God allows us to pass through the Land of Beulah?

The Reason We Need to Pass Through Beulah

First, it is to help us know that we are truly the Lord's delight.

Let's take a look at the depiction of the pilgrims as they enter the Land of Beulah in *The Pilgrim's Progress*.

> "…air was very sweet and pleasant: the way lying directly through it, they enjoyed themselves there for a season. Yea, here they heard continually the singing of birds and saw every day the flowers appear on the earth, and heard the voice of the turtle in the land. In

this country the sun shineth night and day; wherefore this was beyond the Valley of the Shadow of Death, and also out of the reach of Giant Despair; neither could they from this place so much as see Doubting Castle."

The place called the Land of Beulah in *The Pilgrim's Progress* is a land imagined according to Isaiah 62:4.

> "But you will be called Hephzibah, and your land Beulah; for the Lord will take delight in you, and your land will be married."

Hephzibah means "my delight is in Him." If our lives were a continuation of suffering alone, it would not be easy for us to be assured of God's love. However, by experiencing life's blessings season by season, we get to enjoy and appreciate the fact that God truly loves us.

God's confession of love can be expressed as an ontological joy that is grounded in the Creation event. It is a joy comparable to that of parents who finally hold their first baby after the pain of labor. This is also similar to Zephaniah's confession, which we often sing in worship songs.

> "The Lord your God is with you, the Mighty Warrior who saves. He will take great delight in you; in his love he will no longer rebuke you, but will rejoice over you with singing" (Zeph. 3:17).

This joy is comparable to the joy of grandparents who look at their grandchild in love, with nothing to gain. Suk Hee Jung, the author of *On the Things You May Not Remember*, which accounts the story of a grandfather raising his grandson, describes the joy of caring for the grandchildren as the following:

> "Looking after my two grandchildren was an unexpected joy that came to me in my old age like a blossoming spring. Thanks to them, I was filled with precious speculation and speckless communion with them, and I experienced the joy of pure devotion. Now I had someone I could love unreservedly. For the first time in a long time, I felt like I was alive. Just as the sun sets speedily in the evening, it had seemed that the remaining days of my life were racing towards the end. The kids delivered me from withering away. What joy and blessing it is that the end of my life gets a chance to cross the beginning of their life. After meeting you, every moment of my life has been of exuberance, joy, and a blossoming spring."

Wouldn't God the Father's joy as He looks at His children's children be like this? Just as the grandfather experienced joy in the declining stages of his life, God desires His children's children to know that they are His delight, as they pass through the Land of Beulah before they reach heaven.

Second, it is to prepare us as His beautiful bride.
The Bible teaches us that the moment we believe in Jesus, we become his engaged bride. When Jesus returns to this earth, we will participate in the wedding ceremony of Jesus our Lamb as His bride. If so, the lifetime of believers is a preparation to be His bride. Isaiah 62 declares that the Lord is continually at work in us so that we would be worthy in His sight on the day we stand before Him.

> "For Zion's sake I will not keep silent, for Jerusalem's sake I will not remain quiet, till her vindication shines out like the dawn, her salvation like a blazing torch. The nations will see your vindication, and all kings your glory; you will be called by a new name that the mouth of the Lord will bestow" (Isa. 62:1-2).

The Christian doctrine teaches that a believer's lifetime is a process of sanctification. And the moment our sanctification is complete is called glorification. Revelation 21:2 portrays the moment when believers enter into the glory of the completed heaven as the following:

> "I saw the Holy City, the new Jerusalem, coming down out of heaven from God, prepared as a bride beautifully dressed for her husband."

The Lord's zeal for the believers on this earth molds us as His rightful bride. Ephesians 5:25 writes that the Lord loves the church just as a husband loves his wife, and therefore He gave himself up for the church. He shows in the following verses His expectations and ministry for the church, His bride.

> "...to make her holy, cleansing her by the washing with water through the word, and to present her to himself as a radiant church, without stain or wrinkle or any other blemish, but holy and blameless" (Eph. 5:26-27).

Just as the thoughtful groom gives his poor bride luxurious cosmetics to help adorn herself for their wedding day, Jesus gives us

His word to help adorn us for the day when we will stand before Him as His glorious bride. That anticipation is included in the promise of Isaiah 62 where it is written that we will receive a new name, just as Jerusalem will become the New Jerusalem.

> "You will be a crown of splendor in the Lord's hand, a royal diadem in the hand of your God" (Isa. 62:3).

The most precious reason we live on this earth is to finally stand before our Lord one day as His glorious bride, shaped by His hands, and wearing a beautiful, shining crown. This is why the Lord shapes us through suffering in our pilgrimage, but also gives us time to joyfully adorn ourselves for His coming.

Third, it is to help us taste heaven's glory on this earth.

The Land of Beulah is not the New Jerusalem. However, it is where the entire holy city can be seen at a glance. The Land of Beulah is like a preview of the complete heaven that we can experience in advance here on earth. *The Pilgrim's Progress* depicts the Land of Beulah as the following:

> "…for in this land the Shining Ones commonly walked, because

it was upon the borders of heaven. In this land also, the contract between the bride and the bridegroom was renewed; yea, here, "As the bridegroom rejoiceth over the bride, so did their God rejoice over them." (Isa. 62:5) Here they had no want of corn and wine; for in this place they met with abundance of what they had sought for in all their pilgrimage. (Isa. 62:8) Here they heard voices from out of the city, loud voices, saying, "'Say ye to the daughter of Zion, Behold, thy salvation cometh! Behold, his reward is with him!' Here all the inhabitants of the country called them, 'The holy people, The redeemed of the Lord, Sought out'", etc. (Isa. 62:11,12) Now as they walked in this land, they had more rejoicing than in parts more remote from the kingdom to which they were bound; and drawing near to the city, they had yet a more perfect view thereof. It was builded of pearls and precious stones, also the street thereof was paved with gold."

Likewise, there are times when we experience heaven on this earth. Through a joyful church life or when we experience the overflow of God's amazing grace, we often think, "Ah, I feel like I am in Heaven." We can call this the "Beulah experience." It is where we experience the joy of the woman married to the Lord. It is where we experience the following verse: "But you will be called

Hephzibah, and your land Beulah; for the Lord will take delight in you, and your land will be married"(Isa. 62:4).

During the Japanese colonial rule in Korea, Reverend Kwon-Neung Choi(Bong Seok Choi), the evangelist who started "Jesus Salvation, Unbelief Hell" evangelism in Korea, was once caught by Japanese officers. They pressed Rev. Choi by saying, "You preach 'Jesus Salvation, Unbelief Hell.' Then show us where this heaven is!" Then he replied, "I cannot show you the headquarters of heaven as I am not in charge of it. But I can show you a branch of heaven, which is my heart. Heaven is in my heart. All the joy and peace of heaven is here." How biblical is this answer!

In the Beatitudes, Jesus said, "Blessed are the poor in spirit, for theirs is the kingdom of heaven"(Matt. 5:3). When we wholeheartedly believe that Jesus is our King, receive Him as our Lord and obey His Word, we can experience heaven here and now. There is a hymn that only those who believe in Christ and have experienced heaven on earth can sing:

> "Since Christ my soul from sin set free,
> This world has been a Heav'n to me;
> And 'mid earth's sorrows and its woe,
> 'Tis Heav'n my Jesus here to know.(Verse 1)

Once Heaven seemed a far-off place,

Till Jesus showed His smiling face;

Now it's begun within my soul,

'Twill last while endless ages roll.(Verse 2)

What matters where on earth we dwell?

On mountain top or in the dell,

In cottage or a mansion fair,

Where Jesus is 'tis Heaven there.(Verse 3)

O hallelujah, yes, 'tis Heav'n

'Tis Heav'n to know my sins forgiv'n;

On land or sea, what matters where?

Where Jesus is, 'tis Heaven there.(Chorus)"

This is the heavenly hymn that we sing in the Land of Beulah. Depending on our hearts, we can experience the Land of Beulah during our pilgrimage, whenever and wherever. This means that we can experience heaven right here at this moment. And we can sing, "Where Jesus is, 'tis Heaven there." I hope that we will all be pilgrims who sing this song day by day. I hope that we will be heaven's pilgrims who walk the remainder of our life's road, singing praises with joy.

If we encounter our Creator Lord as our Savior and walk with

Him, this praise and confession can become our own. And we will hear the voice of the Lord who calls out to us, "My Hephzibah, my Beulah! My delight is in you."

Questions for the Pilgrimage of Faith

1. What are the three reasons that God allows us to pass through the Land of Beulah?

1)

2)

3)

2. Our lifetime is a process in which we are molded into Christ's rightful bride. What does Jesus our groom do for us, the bride?

3. Have you ever experienced a time when you felt, "Ah, this is Heaven!"?

4. Meditate on how God has transformed your life's grounds into the Land of Beulah and give thanks and praises.

Isaiah 43:1-7

But now, this is what the LORD says -- he who created you, O Jacob, he who formed you, O Israel: "Fear not, for I have redeemed you; I have summoned you by name; you are mine. When you pass through the waters, I will be with you; and when you pass through the rivers, they will not sweep over you. When you walk through the fire, you will not be burned; the flames will not set you ablaze. For I am the LORD, your God, the Holy One of Israel, your Savior; I give Egypt for your ransom, Cush and Seba in your stead. Since you are precious and honored in my sight, and because I love you, I will give men in exchange for you, and people in exchange for your life. Do not be afraid, for I am with you; I will bring your children from the east and gather you from the west. I will say to the north, 'Give them up!' and to the south, 'Do not hold them back.' Bring my sons from afar and my daughters from the ends of the earth -- everyone who is called by my name, whom I created for my glory, whom I formed and made."

Revelations 21:1-2

Then I saw a new heaven and a new earth, for the first heaven and the first earth had passed away, and there was no longer any sea. I saw the Holy City, the new Jerusalem, coming down out of heaven from God, prepared as a bride beautifully dressed for her husband.

Pilgrim's Progress 27

River of Death and New Jerusalem

Are You Ready for the World Beyond Death?

The beloved documentary film, *My Love, Don't Cross That River*, illustrates the moving love story between an elderly couple, a hard sight to see nowadays. The elderly couple is comprised of an 89-year old lady and 98-year old gentleman who wear beautiful hanboks(Korean traditional clothes) and always hold onto each other's hands. In spring, they pick flowers for each other; in summer, they have water fights in the creek; in fall, they play around with the autumn leaves; in winter, they have snow fights.

One day, the grandfather's beloved puppy dies. The elderly couple feels instinctively that the day is coming when they will need to let go of each other's hands and prepare to cross the river. Is that river—the river of parting, the river of death—truly inevitable?

In *The Pilgrim's Progress*, Christian and Hopeful run into the river that blocks the gate and ask two other pilgrims if there is any other way to enter the city. The other pilgrims answer, "You must go through, or you cannot come at the gate."

Christian is troubled and asks again if there is any other way to enter the gate. Then the pilgrims answer, "Yes; but there hath not any save two, to wit, Enoch and Elijah, been permitted to tread that path since the foundation of the world, nor shall until the last trumpet shall sound." Christian and Hopeful look this way and that, but no alternative way could be found to cross the river.

Famous American comedian Johnny Carson once said there are only two certain things in this uncertain world. "Nothing is as certain as death and taxes." He was commenting on America's strict tax system based on the certainty of death.

And rightly so. The probability of death is 100 percent. The author of Ecclesiastes says there is "a time to be born and a time to die" (Eccles. 3:2). Hebrews 9:27 says, "Just as man is destined to die once, and after that to face judgment."

A young man fearful of his father's impending death sought out a monk in the mountains. "Let me know how to prevent my father's death." The monk answered, "Go back to your village and bring me a seed from a house that has never experienced death. Then I will let you know how to prevent your father's death." Obviously the young man could not find such a house.

If we cannot escape from death, we must ask this important question: "Am I ready for the world beyond death?" There are some who believe that there is nothing after death. But as mathematician and philosopher Blaise Pascal says, there is a fifty-fifty chance that there is eternity beyond death. That is why Pascal says, "If God exists and there is life after death, preparing for that is the best bet we can make." Then what preparations must we make to enter the Eternal City after crossing the river of death?

Preparations for Celestial City

First, we must take the certificate that proves that we belong to God.

This is evident as we see Ignorance refused entry into New Jerusalem. Although he approached New Jerusalem, the gates did not open for him, and the men on top of the gate call out to him saying, "You may not enter the gate without your certificate, and cannot see the King." The certificate was proof that one belonged to God.

Isaiah 43:1 lays out three important steps for one to become part of God's people.

> "But now, this is what the LORD says - he who created you, O Jacob, he who formed you, O Israel: 'Fear not for I have redeemed you; I have summoned you by name; you are mine.'"

Here we see three important keywords that make us become people of God: "created," "redeemed," and "summoned." These three ministries belong to the Triune God.

First, God the Father "created" us. We are his creation. Then Jesus the Son came to "redeem" us who had fallen into sin and departed from our Creator God by paying the price of His blood on the cross and restoring us to become God's people again. And God the Spirit "summoned" us from among many people to come to Jesus, believe, and accept him as our Lord, marking a seal upon us to confirm that we belong to God.

Do you believe in this truth? This faith that believes in God as Creator, Savior, and Lord is our certificate.

Let us remember the demise of Ignorance. The last paragraph of *The Pilgrim's Progress* ends in this way:

> "Then said they, 'Have you none?' But the man answered never a word. So they told the King; but He would not come down to see him, but commanded the two Shining Ones that conducted Christian and Hopeful to the City, to go out and take Ignorance, and bind him hand and foot, and have him away. Then they took him up, and carried him through the air to the door that I saw in the side of the hill, and put him in there. Then I saw that there was a way to hell, even from the gates of heaven, as well as from the City of Destruction!"

This description most likely is inspired by the parable of the unprepared guest at the wedding banquet in Matthew 22, who was kicked out because he was not wearing wedding clothes.

> "He asked, 'How did you get in here without wedding clothes, friend?' The man was speechless. Then the king told the attendants, 'Tie him hand and foot, and throw him outside, into the

darkness, where there will be weeping and gnashing of teeth. For many are invited, but few are chosen'"(Matt. 22:12-14).

The wedding clothes in the parable are described as a certificate in *The Pilgrim's Progress*. The grace sinners receive when they place their faith in Christ and are forgiven of their sins and called righteous-- this grace is the wedding clothes we must wear to take part in the heavenly party. Are your wedding clothes ready? Is your certificate that proves you belong to God ready? We must examine ourselves.

Second, we must anticipate "God's presence" that is with us even in the River of Death.

In *The Pilgrim's Progress*, after confirming there is no other way to Celestial City, Christian and Hopeful set foot into the River of Death. Not long after, Christian loses his senses in fear. This shows us that crossing the River of Death was no easy task for him.

Hopeful, Christian's companion, shouts that he must believe that Jesus is with him and that He makes us whole through the waters. Then Christian regains his senses and says, "I remember He said that He is with me." The Word Christian remembers is the promise written in Isaiah 43:2:

> "When you pass through the waters, I will be with you; and when you pass through the rivers, they will not sweep over you. When you walk through the fire, you will not be burned; the flames will not set you ablaze."

Then something remarkable happens. As Christian trusts that the Lord's presence is with Him, the deep river becomes shallow. He finds solid ground for his feet to stand on. And he finally reaches the bank of the river on the other side. Two Shining Ones come to walk with Christian and Hopeful towards the city gate.

Indeed, just like the psalmist declared, "Even though I walk through the valley of the shadow of death, I will fear no evil, for you are with me" (Ps. 23:40), God is present not only in the Valley of the Shadow of Death, but also in the River of Death. The one who promised that "surely I am with you always, to the very end of the age" kept His word, coming to the pilgrims crossing the River of Death.

Third, we must look forward to the glorious city on the other side of the river.

With the help of the angels, Christian and Hopeful arrive at the gate. They knock on the gate and show their certificates as they were instructed. The gates swing open, and as they cross over, their appearance transforms. They are dressed in garments that shine like gold. There are people with harps and crowns waiting for them. The bells ring with joy, and there is a loud voice that tells the pilgrims to "enter into the joy of your Lord!"

The brightly shining city comes into view. People with crowns on their heads are holding palms in their hands and singing praise with golden harps. There are winged angels among them, praising without ceasing that "Holy, holy, holy is the Lord!" Finally, the pilgrims had arrived in New Jerusalem, the celestial city.

Now see how the Bible describes New Jerusalem.

> "Then I saw a new heaven and a new earth, for the first heaven and the first earth had passed away, and there was no longer any sea. I saw the Holy City, the new Jerusalem, coming down out of heaven from God, prepared as a bride beautifully dressed for her husband" (Rev. 21:1-2).

Does this not remind you of the famous hymn written by Frederick E. Weatherly and Stephen Adams titled "The Holy City"?

> "Last night I lay a-sleeping there came a dream so fair / I stood in

old Jerusalem beside the temple there / I heard the children singing, and ever as they sang / Methought the voice of angels from heaven in answer rang / ⋯ And all who would might enter, and no one was denied / No need of moon or stars by night; or sun to shine by day / It was the new Jerusalem that would not pass away."

Our journey of faith is the march that looks ahead to this glorious city. And finally we have arrived at the destination. If we walk the pilgrimage with eyes of faith to see the city of glory ahead of us, we will be eternally grateful that we did not give up no matter how deep the River of Death was and finally crossed to the other side.

What will we experience after arriving at this city? The promise of the Word of God says the following:

> "He will wipe every tear from their eyes. There will be no more death or mourning or crying or pain, for the old order of things has passed away" (Rev. 21:4).

Now that we have crossed the dark river, we stand on the shiny hill of New Jerusalem. We will now wipe our tears and sing John W. Peterson's "Jesus Led Me All the Way" with great thanksgiving and joy.

"Someday life's journey will be o'er

and I shall reach that distant shore

I'll sing while entr'ing Heaven's door

Jesus led me all the way.(Verse 1)

If God should let me there review

the winding paths of earth I knew

It would be proven clear and true

Jesus led me all the way.(Verse 2)

And hither to my Lord has led today

He guides each step I tread

And soon in Heav'n it will be said

Jesus led me all the way.(Verse 3)

Jesus led me all the way led me step by step each day

I will tell the saints and angels as I lay my burdens down

Jesus led me all the way.(Chorus)"

I hope that on that day we will all meet on that hill and sing this praise together. I pray none of us will be left behind because we do not have the certificate that proves we belong to God. I pray that we will be true and faithful pilgrims to walk this road in faith, cross the final River of Death, and praise the One seated on the throne in glory on the shiny hill.

Questions for the Pilgrimage of Faith

1. What must we prepare to cross the River of Death and enter the eternal city?

1)

2)

3)

2. Describe the certificate of heaven. Do you have this certificate?

3. How does the Bible and John Bunyan's *The Pilgrim's Progress* describe heaven?

4. Talk about how you are preparing for death and your hope for heaven.

Notes

1. Rev. Sun Joo Gil was the first Korean to be ordained as a Presbyterian minister and considered the Father of Korean Christianity.
2. Rev. Sung Bong Lee was a powerful revival preacher in Korea during the Japanese occupation and after liberation.
3. Pilgrim House is a retreat center in Gapyeong, Korea operated by Global Mission Church.
4. MV Sewol, a passenger ferry from Incheon to Jeju, capsized and sank on the morning of April 16, 2014. A total of 304 passengers and crew members died in the disaster.

Controversy arose as Byeong Eun Yoo, the founder of the Salvation Sect and de facto owner of the ferry's operating firm, was connected to the sinking.